THE RESONANT LIFE

Elizabeth A. Baker

Copyright © 2018 Elizabeth A. Baker

All rights reserved. No part of this publication may be reproduced, distributed, or transmitted in any form or by any means, including photocopying, recording, or other electronic or mechanical methods, without the prior written permission of the publisher, except in the case of brief quotations embodied in critical reviews and certain other noncommercial uses permitted by copyright law.

Printed in the United States of America

First Printing, 2018

ISBN 9781728849652

Independently Published
www.elizabethabaker.com

To those who wander and those who wonder, everything is new, every breath begets new possibility, and every step is a new journey unfolding.

ABOUT THE AUTHOR

Celebrated for her "terrifying dynamic range," cleanliness of sound, as well as unique sensitivity and ability to sculpt her performance for the acoustics of a space, Elizabeth A. Baker is a dramatic performer with an honest, near psychic connection to music, which resounds with audiences of all ages and musical backgrounds. As a creator, her understanding of sonic space from organic intuition and studies in music production, pair with a unique eclectic voice, making for a spatial and auditory experience of music. Eschewing the collection of traditional titles that describe single elements of her body of work, Elizabeth refers to herself as a "New Renaissance Artist" that embraces a constant stream of change and rebirth in practice, which expands into a variety of media, chiefly an exploration of how sonic and spatial worlds can be manipulated to personify a variety of philosophies and principles both tangible as well as intangible.

An active performer highly sought after for her unique concert presentation methods, which break the fourth wall and draw the audience further into the music by asking them to listen beyond the surface through interactive dialogue, reminding them that there is no such thing as an incorrect interpretation of a work. Elizabeth firmly believes that every person will encounter music in a unique manner because each person comes from a different set of cultural norms, life experiences, and even the way they physically hear can be a factor to consider when seeking to relate with a work. Her solo performances have featured engagements at Lamar University (Beaumont, TX), Flying Monkey Arts Collective (Huntsville, AL), Eyedrum (Atlanta, GA), Southern Methodist University (Dallas, TX), Georgia Museum of Art (Athens, GA), Café Resonance (Montreal, QC), Timucua Arts Foundation (Orlando, FL), Center for New Music (San Francisco, CA), and the Good Shepherd Chapel (Seattle, WA). As a mixed media movement performer her collaborative work has been presented at The Joslyn Museum of Art (Omaha, NE), The Gallery at Avalon Island (Orlando, FL) as well as at St. Petersburg Opera (Saint Petersburg, FL).

Emmy-award winning composer Larry Groupé has referred to her works as "Perfect." and compared one of her early works to Debussy's Engulfed Cathedral. Elizabeth's works have been featured by performers, programming organisations, and online publications including: Composers Circle, I Care If You Listen, TEDxYouthTampaBay (Tampa, FL), Tenth Intervention (NYC), Verdant Vibes (Providence, RI), OME Festival (Phoenix, AZ), Voic(ed) Project (Chicago, IL), The Florida Orchestra (Tampa Bay, FL), The Furies (Los Angeles, CA) as well as at Electronic Music Midwest Festival, and the 19th International Festival of Women Composers. Her compositions and work as an arts advocate have been studied in academic institutions throughout the United States including USC-Thornton, University of Buffalo, Wichita State University, and the University of Georgia – Athens.

In 2015 she received an Individual Artist Award from the St. Petersburg Arts Alliance and the City of Saint Petersburg, Florida to create and present an original sound installation In Our Own Words: A Sonic Memory Quilt, which told the stories of various African-Americans in a fresh avant-garde manner, framed by evolving drones and a four-hour live performance by Elizabeth. Additional honours include, a 2017 Professional Artist Fellowship from Creative Pinellas; a guest artist spot in the inaugural co-incidence residency in Somerville, MA with master resident Michael Pisaro, who described her compositions as a marriage Schoenberg, Cage, and Satie; as well as a 2017 Individual Artist Award from the St. Petersburg Arts Alliance.

In addition to her work on the concert stage and on the page, writing for other performing artists, Elizabeth has extensive training in recording arts, live sound reinforcement, and consistently received praise as well as high marks for the artistic sensibility and technical excellence of her mixes at St. Petersburg College, where she studied closely under mastering engineer Dave Greenberg. Today, friends and colleagues across the globe, frequently look to her as a consultant on projects for her skills as both a recording and mix engineer.

Combining her love of electronics and keyboard instruments, Elizabeth embarked on a mission in 2015 to promote works for toy piano and electronics, using a setup that combines handmade microphones and hydrophones. Her original works have been hailed by the Orlando Weekly as "a sterling testimonial to her artistry that proves she's not just an expert in the toy piano field but a pioneer." In Fall 2015, **Schoenhut Piano Company** added Elizabeth A. Baker to their official artist roster.

Between 2016 and 2017, Elizabeth began working extensively with dancers on a number of projects including works for film, stage, and workshops which primarily featured toy piano, electronics, and Indian harmonium, a keyboard instrument that rarely appears on the Western musical concert stage. With the support of her mover colleagues and friends, Elizabeth began incorporating movement in her own performances, adding new depth to her interdisciplinary practice. In 2017 **Source Audio LLC**, officially endorsed Elizabeth for her innovative work creating musical compositions through physical choreography using their Hot Hands USB Wireless MIDI Controller technology.

A sensitive improviser, with experience in a wide array of genres, Elizabeth is a frequent collaborator for improvisational ensembles and performances throughout North America, and maintains three active improvisation duos with artists **Robert Hess** (Toronto, ON), **Leo Suarez** (Philadelphia, PA) and **Nathan Corder** (Oakland, CA).

Elizabeth is author of *Toyager: A Toy Piano Method*, the first comprehensive instructional book for toy piano, featuring principles of technique, practice strategies, music notation, as well as improvisational tactics. Additional books include a multimedia collection of writings and photographs called *Musings of a Young Composer* and *Compositions for the Contemporary Student Pianist*, an anthology of solo piano pieces. As a solo artist, Elizabeth has self-released numerous albums including: **{this is not a piano album}** (2016), **A Series of Strange Narratives** (2015), **A Sonic Memory Quilt** (2015), **Music for Possible Probable Ghost Listeners** (2015), **{BAGGAGE CLAIM}** (2015), and **Solo Piano Compositions In Recital** (2011). In 2017, Elizabeth signed with California-based **Aerocade Music**, her first release on the label, **Quadrivium** was released in May 2018 to rave reviews. In late-2018 Elizabeth published first motivational book **The Resonant Life: Attack. Decay. Sustain. Release. Resonate.** is inspired by personal experiences in the music industry, life lessons, anecdotal stories, and methods for navigating the road of success. It breaks down key aspects of life and relates them to the fundamental parts of sound. Through mirroring the sculpture of ADSR (Attack. Decay. Sustain. Release.) in an analogue synthesiser environment, Elizabeth presents an overall technique of personalised growth for others in all sectors of their life.

As an experimental filmmaker, her work has been shown at festivals including Women of the Lens (United Kingdom), and the African Smartphone International Film Festival (Nigeria).

Elizabeth is founder of The New Music Conflagration, Inc., a nonprofit created to promote the work of contemporary composers and musicians. She is also, founder of the Florida International Toy Piano Festival. In March 2018, amid growing success with regard to her solo career, Elizabeth retired from nonprofit arts management to fully pursue her artistic endeavours. Elizabeth still remains committed to new music promotion and community by presenting experimental music workshops across the North American continent. elizabethabaker.com

FOREWARD

What makes a piano sing, an orchestral hall swell, a bar venue performance fill your bones? Resonance, the physical principles which govern how one small unit, a basic vibration (in music we call this a fundamental tone) is expanded and passed into other, often larger vibrational bodies. Resonance has an electric momentum, though we frequently associate it with the amplification of acoustic instruments, if you speak to sound artists and engineers they will talk about their fascination and sometimes frustration with the natural resonant frequencies that occur in any given space that isn't an anechoic chamber.

As a person who has been captivated by sound for her whole life, the concept of a single nexus, that from the point of its creation has almost limitless possibilities for where it can spread and how much it can be amplified, has always peaked my interest. Consider that every musical work begins in essence with a single sound. Once a single point of vibrational energy has been released into the ether, it has from both the compositional standpoint as well as a physics-informed sonic exploration viewpoint, a vast but finite web of possibility for expansion; and this ideal parallels profoundly the fundamental aspects of human experience. We are born into this world with a sea of possibilities within a smattering of fixed realities, all of which parallel the physical qualities and artistic sensibilities a kin to the creation and performance of music. Our lives are wrought with indeterminacy, a principle fundamental to both quantum theory and advanced studies of contemporary music theory. We improvise daily and discover new things through improvisation. We interpret various manuscripts in the form of books, media, manuals, laws, and general rules that govern our roles in society. Our actions touch others effecting change, similar to the way that a countermelody or the addition of instruments in a chamber ensemble deepen and expand the sonic palette available to everyone as a communal unity. Our words lead others down paths both internal as well as external… the same way a text score or a graphic score can be interpreted in a variety of ways by a sea of different artists – whereby each individual will have unique internalised relationships with the same experimental score, a third party analysing the performance data of all artists in the pool of possibility, will discover over time, a general trend of intersecting external interpretations of the score.

Our existence is a fundamental vibration, and this book is about exploring the structure of your natural harmonic signature and realising your fundamental purpose, so that you can maximise the resonance of your voices and actions in the world. A resonant life is more than just following your purpose path, it is about learning how to live consciously and positively in a manner that allows your energy to fill the Earth in the same manner that a violin solo consumes an entire concert hall, reaching the patrons at the very back of the room to touch their hearts with as much impact as the personal and intimate experience felt by the audience members in the first few rows of the hall.

I have always been a heavy proponent of deep thinking and questioning the issues set before me. This book is not to be taken as canon, but rather an invitation to look within yourself and to evaluate your strengths, places for growth, and how you can foster a meaningful living legacy that impacts the world around you. I have packed this book with a good amount of anecdotal stories, in addition to my analysis of specific ideals; but each chapter includes sections for you to ruminate on the issues presented in the text and how they apply to your life. I highly encourage you to keep notes in this book and to procure a journal where you can document your thoughts and musings as you embark on this journey of self-discovery.

Delving into the depths of your own ethics, psyche, and purpose is not an easy task; it takes work to approach yourself with a mind open enough to question your habits and break away from the pack mentality embedded in our modern culture. Before we venture further down the rabbit hole, I want you to take a moment to recognise the strength of character you have to even consider reading this book and considering the contents within; and I want you to acknowledge this inner fortitude when things become challenging along the way.

My father has always said this to me throughout my life, "Elizabeth, remember that old African proverb. How do you eat an elephant? One bite at a time." Dearest reader, with every word you absorb and every page you turn, every musing you write, and every thought you turnover in your mind; you are taking a bite, and before you know it, the whole elephant will be consumed!

In line with our analysis of how the sonic arts and life experience rooted in the arts contain profound lessons, that can expand or rather resonate to other areas of our lives – this book is arranged in accordance to the parts of a single sound wave - Attack, Decay, Sustain, Release, and the last one, which I have added for purposes of this text Resonate.

The reader will find a great degree of what we call in the recording industry "bleed" – a common event that happens commonly when one is recording with multiple microphones – no matter how high-quality the microphones are, when several instrumentalists and/or vocalists are in a room and asked to play together – you are going to hear some of the piano in the cello mic and the same will be true for the rest of the various close microphones on other areas of the ensemble. In this book, topics will often bleed into other chapters in a non-linear fashion, because there are many lessons that can be gleaned from a singular occurrence or particular individual.

In analogue synthesis one is in control of the parameters of a sound wave, altering the length of any one of the parts of sound Attack, Decay, Sustain, Release (ADSR) changes the colour and character of a sound. You are the architect of your sound, in this book and you may find that you want to spend more time in one section and have a shorter time in another, all of this is part of the journey and the sculpting of your signature sound as it resounds through the universe.

ATTACK

NOTHING IS IMPOSSIBLE
MOVING FORWARD DESPITE NAYSAYERS
& LEARNING TO DREAM BIG

I am not one to tell people that their dreams or goals are unrealistic. I learned along time ago that life can lead us into very unexpected places and on paths that we never even imagined possible. A difficult lesson that came to me early in my career is – the people that you think should have your back, the people that you trust, are often the ones who will knock you off your feet with how quickly they want to curb and limit the scope of your dreams.

While I was studying music at the collegiate level, I participated in a summer vocal workshop where the head of the program told me, very publicly before a recital, that I had no career in music ahead of me. During my undergraduate studies as a classical guitar major, I had multiple teachers outside of my studio stating that I didn't have the work ethic to make it in the music industry. After my traditional music studies, I went to commercial music school, one of the lead professors called me into his office before class while the rest of the students were outside the door to tell me that I would never be successful because I didn't have the people skills to make it. I briefly worked for a summer music festival, where the founder of the program stated that while I might have had some small talent, I lacked the technique or potential to ever truly make anything happen.

Before the present commercial music program even existed at St. Petersburg College, it was basically forbidden to have a rock concert on campus. When I entered college as a dual enrolled student in the spring of 2006, the president of St. Petersburg College ruled with a conservative iron fist that made certain musical expression, difficult or near impossible to present on any of the campuses. I sought to change that and produce the first rock concert on the St. Petersburg/Gibbs campus, in 2007. Through a lot of meetings and assurances, I was able to book four groups for a rock concert in the gymnasium. From a sheer attendance perspective, the event was a flop – there were more police officers at the event, as a precaution requested by the college president, than actual audience members. The acoustics of a space designed for basketball games with all of the stereotypical slapjack and muddy reverb are on the whole, less than stellar for any sort of music, especially "rock" music. However, this event proved that music outside the traditional classical and jazz lexicon could exist at the college, and nothing was going to be destroyed – this simple act of organised revolution spearheaded by a single determined student, gave the music faculty fodder for the case to establish a world-class commercial music program at St. Petersburg College. Today, the Music Industry & Recording Arts (MIRA) program at St. Petersburg College has made access to state-of-the art gear and innovative recording arts training affordable and accessible to the local community. Alumni from the MIRA program include successful working studio engineers, live sound engineers, performing artists, and gear designers. After self-releasing several albums while in MIRA and after my capstone for the program; I signed with Meerenai Shim's boutique-label, Aerocade Music in the fall of 2017. In discussions about my first album on the label, I made it clear that I wanted to have the engineering done by my former classmates Greg Lacompte and Melissa Harris Chambers. I felt that if I was being given an opportunity to take my career to the next level, I wanted to share the resultant opportunities with people that were not only highly skilled but who believed in me and deserved a shot at something with a different reach beyond their typical projects. Today, I read glowing reviews of the album and I feel proud of the work that Melissa and Greg did to make my two-hour concept into a full on immersive experience. This is an example of the resonant life in action, one fundamental tone amplified, surrounded and supported by it's harmonic counterparts enacting changes bigger than the sum of their individual parts.

In this modern age, hurtful words and suppression of your dreams don't always come in the form of people who pull you aside and to deliver a barrage of dehumanising commentary to your face. Unfortunately, the dreadful reality is that on your purpose driven success path you will encounter people who cowardly hide behind snide Internet comments and lengthy biting hate emails – some directed to you alone, and others that copy people on their correspondence, whom they feel will be key allies in the systematic destruction of your reputation. While one would think that cyberbullying is something that adults have the common decency to refrain from pursuing; I can attest to the personal receipt of lengthy emails (some as long as ten printed single-spaced pages) telling me that I am a horrible person, that I have no artistic merit, that I don't deserve to succeed, that my career is not fiscally viable, and worst of all messages that widen the focus of their attacks to include my loved ones. While I fervently believe in constructive criticism as a healthy part of positive growth; the credible strength of a critical source is inherently corrupted when feelings of jealousy are wrought within malicious sentiments expressed to another human being, under the guise of professional critique.

The fundamental common thread in all of the negative feedback instances I've mentioned thus far, is that each one of the individuals doling out criticisms did not see the path ahead of me or even see me as a beautiful celestial creative sentient being. Their version of success or "making it" in the music industry remains one that is far from the reality that I experience today; but it wasn't their place to attempt to quash my dreams with well-meaning albeit, misplaced advice. None of us are architects of the cosmos; and there are miracles always waiting to be revealed around each sinuous curve of spacetime. I am steadfast in the position that all the time anyone spends in trying to put others down and humiliate them, is time and effort that should be simply devoted to improving their craft; converting surplus negative energy into positive actions; and ultimately moving forward with grace. When we try to tear others down, when we try to suppress their rise to the top; we are the most ugly versions of ourselves. When we help others over the wall, when we breakdown barriers that have been set in place by generations of prejudiced gatekeepers, when we use our influence to inspire others; we are shining beacons of light wrapped in love and our purposeful actions resonate beyond our beings.

We are all meant to be successful, but success frequently evades us when we stray from our purpose path. I'll say it again one more time for the people in the back, WE ARE ALL MEANT TO BE SUCCESSFUL! This life was not meant to be one full of perpetual misery. We are here to find some fulfilment through personal and professional development over the course of our time on this plane of existence. We are all meant to be successful. We are all unique and wonderful celestial beings. Our unhappiness, which often leads to a sea of destructive behaviours that bring harm to ourselves as well as others (examples include substance abuse, physical abuse of others, psychological abuse, self-harm, overexercising, overspending, eating disorders, etc.), is a direct product of forgetting that we are radiant sentient beings with purpose.

Sometimes the person creating the tallest hurdle to realising the potential of our ability to dream big and follow our purpose path is… us. As a child, I was always a planner. I was going to become a constitutional lawyer who fervently advocated for the reduction of corruption in our political system… at least that is what I told the outside world. In truth, I have always had a passion for equity and justice; however, from age four, I had actively expressed behind closed doors, an interest in being the conductor of an orchestra. I started writing music as soon as I had a piano of my own and the ability to scrawl stemless ovals in my little manuscript book. I would improvise at the piano for hours upon hours, even though my Russian teacher slapped my hands when I deviated from the written notes in my red covered Thompson piano method book during weekly lessons. It was here, that my penchant for perseverance and lateral thinking began to bubble to the surface. It was also here that seeds of doubt and expectation were planted, growing into sizeable fruit espousing that if I couldn't perfectly interpret the things in front of my face and conform with a set of rigid rules set forth by centuries of old dead white men; I had no place in music. After informing my parents that I didn't feel as though I was benefiting from the structure imposed on my lessons, I left my Russian piano teacher, and still kept practicing and writing on my own. The music that I primarily composed in middle school were pieces that became things that for my ears alone, and I felt shame to play in public. I was so afraid to share my music with others that I often hurriedly shut the piano and pretended to be working on another task whenever I heard the garage door go up to signal the arrival of one or both of my parents. I spent my middle school years with glints of my love for the arts peaking through piles of alternate labels and interests – I pursued my talents for dance, eventually trading dance for the practical path of a track star… or at least something that would pay my way through college. I lived my childhood largely in a place of fear about pursuing my artistic voice because I came from a family, but primarily a community where conventional success and traditional thinking were highly prized. I went to a private Roman Catholic high school where more money was spent on football and basketball than on academics; a school where the drama program lacked as much of a diverse population as the rest of the school. I remember feeling perpetually ostracised in chorus, because I didn't have the angelic voice or porcelain doll aesthetic of the skinny white girls. Several of these all-American white girls went on to follow their passion with the supportive encouragement that had been foundational for them during high school, to have careers as working actresses on television and Broadway. High school became a time when I became hyper aware that being a black woman in America, put me in a specific role... I was meant to be a track star and to get a full-ride scholarship to a Division I school. I had college scouts at my track meets from the time I was a sophomore in high school, offering very enticing things from schools with huge names and piles of money behind them... and my private track coach was hoping that my name would be among the ranks of the great US Olympians. I fell in line... I did what was expected... I took honours classes... I broke school and county records on the tarmac... I stuck to the plan... I enjoyed the feeling of crossing the finish line first and turning around to see my other competitors getting to the line way after me... I hid the light of my musical talents under a giant bushel basket, thinking that it would eventually become a manageable flame or completely extinguish.

And so, just as there were people who would discourage me from moving forward with my artistic maturation, in the early days of my musical journey their was doubts were within my own mind as well. The crippling doubt that held in the blocks at the starting line of my artistic journey, continued until my senior year of high school, when for some cosmic reason a switch flipped and I knew unequivocally, I was meant to spend my life in the world of sonic exploration. I didn't have a plan, and though I strongly felt a calling towards the world of sound. I was torn and lost, until one day; I stopped doubting myself, and began trusting that if I looked carefully enough, there would be a path in the overgrown jungle of possibility that someone had already marked with their machete as they'd cut their way through years before.

Few people know that I started my formal collegiate music career as a classical guitar performance major. These days I frequently make the joke that majoring in classical guitar performance is equivalent to a college major in underwater basketweaving; and furthermore, all former classical guitar majors end up playing music in complex meters in experimental projects at remote venues that you can't find on Google Maps. Considering the wide array of DIY venues and my penchant for asymmetrical meters that have been a part of my evolution, the "joke" is a fairly accurate statement on the trajectory of someone who pursues classical guitar performance as a major. Blissfuly unaware of the limited prospects, at the time I entered college, majoring in guitar was the seemingly logical choice, because I was playing guitar in an all-girl indie rock band and writing my own songs for that band, as well as composing the weekly Responsorial psalms for the contemporary choir at the Roman Catholic Church across the street from my childhood home. I famously carried my guitar with me to every class in senior year of high school, and negotiated my way out of class time so I could practice guitar in the halls during the school day. Negotiation and lateral thinking got me into quite a bit of hot water during my high school times, but it was here that my fire for questioning and conceptual expression begun to expand. In my senior year, apart from carrying my acoustic guitar around to every class, I was reading Descartes and the writings of Henry G. Frankfurt – I believed that "please" was an overused social courtesy that ultimately made many things optional. One fall afternoon, my English teacher told us at that she would be going away at the end of the week and that we would have an assignment on the story *Sir Gawain and the Green Knight*, and specified that we "please" take the time to read it before class that Friday. Of course, by my logic, "Please read before Friday" meant, "you can read this on Friday, if you wish." Now, Friday was my agreed upon day to sit outside English class and practice guitar, so I wasn't very happy when I finally opened my Literature book at the end of the week to find that the story was much longer than I could read in a fifty minute class period AND write a full-page essay about with time to spare for guitar practice... so lateral thinking, and some good old-fashioned imagination came into play. Our English teacher had left a prompt on the board for our essay, "Is Sir Gawain a hero? Why or why not?" I could have walked away defeated, but this essay was for a grade... and I wanted to get my precious practice time in, so I skimmed through the story and set to writing what I consider to be one of my greatest thesis statements of my entire life… "Sir Gawain is not a hero because a hero is a sandwich, and Sir Gawain is neither tasty nor edible because he is a mythical mercenary construct." I later went on to expand on how the Green Knight represented environmental organisations, while Sir

Gawain was clearly an agent for corporate special interest groups. In Social Justice class, I used the teacher's own syllabus as defence for my argument that she had not achieved her goal of allowing us the space to question issues of social import, and that by her use of subjective materials, subjective questioning, and indoctrinating propaganda in an attempt to make us regurgitate answers that aligned with her own personal mores; she had not only negated the course objectives approved by our parents, school administration, and the certification boards, but she had abandoned the definitive spirit of the term social justice entirely. I spent a lot of time in the teacher's lounge eating snacks because I was consistently kicked out of class for questioning the ethics of her indoctrination… I mean, teaching methods.

Meanwhile, the spark for questioning the philosophical structure of the world around me and using personal analyses to inform my actions yielded, hours in the office negotiating peace treaties betwixt me and various school authorities. This fundamental flow of question, analyse, and informed action, resonated within my being at such a fever pitched vibration that my lifestyle grew into one by which, I actively held myself accountable for the investment of time and energy that I put towards my musical studies, as well as the principle of constant check-ins and self-analysis that would become a part of my mature artistic practice. I woke up with the sun and drove to school, so I could practice in solitude before everyone arrived.

Dreams have a funny way of taking hold and redirecting you. In my last months as an undergrad classical guitar performance major, I kept having recurring dreams where I could see myself performing on a stage in a concert hall for many people. The catch? In every one of these dreams I was performing on a piano, instead of a classical guitar. Piano had been my first instrument. My mum had taken me to an orchestral performance of Peter and the Wolf when I was about three years old, after which I declared gallantly to my parents that, "I want to be the man with the stick." As my mum was raised in England and had worked at the Royal Opera House in her youth, her first instinct a year later when I had worn out at least three copies of the London Philharmonic's rendition of Peter and the Wolf and could isolate each instrument's part from wrote – it was here that my piano lessons and first true entree into the musical world as a practitioner began at age four.

As an undergrad, I was required to take piano lessons but never officially declared a secondary major in piano. I was so hyper-focused on guitar that my piano practice was sloppy and not as regimented as my guitar practice. While I wasn't someone who was blessed with perfect pitch to A-440, I have always had pretty good relative pitch, which I would argue is a more useful tool when switching between styles, ensembles, and historical instruments because A-440 and equal temperament are only modern regional standards... but I digress. I spent a lot of my early undergraduate piano lessons relying upon relative pitch to guide me through pieces, which meant that I wasn't rehearsing with a metronome, which meant that my rhythm was inconsistent and I relied heavily on the pull and push of time that we refer to in music as rubato – I generally sustained notes for the lengths that were relative to each other and approximate to the notation on the pager, but not quite exact. My primary piano professor during my undergrad training was an amazing Columbian-born pianist, who would later go on to achieve the one of the most prestigious sponsorships in the world as an official Steinway Artist, and travel the world breathing new life into works from the pianoforte repertoire of Western mainstays such as Bach and Mozart. He was an unconventional piano teacher, always willing to tailor his pedagogy to individual students' needs and personalities. Some of the exercises he prescribed included switching a standard piano bench for a yoga ball to assist with feeling rhythm through my body as I played, and placing noise-cancelling headphones over my ears during lessons so that I couldn't use my ears to cheat. One day, he finally lost it with my refusal to practice piano with a metronome but instead of screaming or putting me down like other teachers might, he told me a story, one that I haven't forgotten and one that I will share with you dear reader; however, my retelling won't be as fanciful, because it doesn't include the live sound track that my professor improvised at the piano as he wove this delightful story for me:

> "Once upon a time, there was a young woman named Elizabeth and she took piano lessons. Every week she would show up for her lessons, get her books out, sit on the piano bench, and her piano teacher would ask 'Did you practice with the metronome this week?'

And every week Elizabeth would hang her head and look down and say, 'No, professor, I did not practice with the metronome this week.' So one day, Elizabeth went home and put the metronome underneath her pillow and went to sleep – and while she was sleeping THE RHYTHM FAIRY APPEARED with a beautiful flowing sparkly gown, that was covered with eighth notes, and quarter notes, AND EVEN RESTS! The Rhythm Fairy waved her magical wand, and all of Elizabeth's rhythm problems went away!"

I want to say that after this incident I was completely dedicated to my piano studies, but the truth is that while I did make more of an effort to practice; I wasn't perfect and classical guitar was still my primary obsession. It wasn't until the nagging recurring dreams kept insisting that I reevaluate my path, that I begun to shift my focus back to the piano, and in refocusing on my first instrument there was an immediate and noticeable transference of obsessive energy from the guitar to the piano. In many ways, this transference of energy went largely unchecked because I was the only classical guitar performance major in the guitar studio at my four-year college, I kept strange hours and often practiced when other students were in large ensemble or super-late at night when the rest of the department was off having fun with each other.

At the same time my dreams about being a concert pianist were fermenting under the surface, I was still playing at bars, sketchy DIY venues, and house shows. My dream always occurred in a fancy concert hall, me dressed in a beautiful black gown with crystals, under stage lights that offered the sort of homey glow that I generally attribute to the soft yellow hues of an exposed Edison bulb or Himalayan salt lamp – all of this was in direct opposition to the reality of the moment. I didn't know how I would make that dream into a reality, but it remained at the forefront of my consciousness, reoccurring until September 22, 2011. It was on that September evening amidst a torrential downpour that is ever so common in Florida during hurricane season, when St. Petersburg College did a large scale concert of my solo piano compositions and the first time I stepped out on stage in a black concert gown, walked to a concert grand Steinway, sat down, and felt undeniable energy connections not only with the artisanal crafted mass of metal and wood in front of me but also, with the notes that dispersed into the ether, another worldly presence, and a strong sense of the emotional journeys that the people in the audience went on as they stepped into my sonic world for a moment. This was the day that I reset my trip odometer on my purpose path. This was the day that I felt I was heading in the right direction. This was the day that I truly stopped looking back.

People often tell me that they are in awe with how I just continue to move forward, to dream bigger, and to keep executing. I say that nothing is impossible. I say that if you trust in your abilities, if you trust in your purpose; the right opportunities will present themselves. Moreover, if you put in the work, you will be prepared to perform at optimum potential when opportunities of importance present themselves to you.

Opportunities sometimes have to be created to make those big dreams of yours into reality. The concert that I mentioned above was not an opportunity that existed before I asked my piano professor, the academic chair, the dean of the department, and the provost of the campus for permission to do a concert that featured my piano works in such a massive manner. I had to rally the support of the entire piano department, present piano students, as well as alumni, in order to source performers for the concert. I had to make schedules, have a rubric for current piano students who were doing the concert for class credit, assemble a jury to evaluate student progress, print scores, discuss a vision for the entire event, design posters, and among other tasks proof programs. All of these efforts in pursuit of a smooth professional evening of presenting my work to the community, started in a simple practice room at a less than stellar upright piano with a mustard yellow mechanical pencil, manuscript paper, practice sessions that began at dawn, only to be interrupted by classes, and only to end when the security guards had to lock up the building for the evening. It was an endeavour that no student had done before me, and one that has yet to be matched to this day.

Achieving your dreams is one of the most addictive highs that doesn't have any clinical downsides, and once you make one seemingly impossible task a reality, you just keep dreaming bigger... but it starts with that first dream. As absurd as it sounds, step one of the dream to that large-scale concert in a beautiful hall on an exquisitely powerful concert grand piano, was moving from rehearsing on the well-worn upright pianos in practice rooms with windows where other students could distract me, to classrooms with grand pianos away from the nexus of gossip and drama that make up any music department practice room block or average work place break room. Changing my working environment, changed my attitude towards my work because my time in the rooms with grand pianos was limited by classroom schedules, I immediately became more serious about my craft and viewed the time I spent honing my technique as a precious gift not to be squandered. When we change the narrative in our minds about how we see ourselves and our goals, we make space for bigger dreams.

NOTHING IS IMPOSSIBLE
MOVING FORWARD DESPITE NAYSAYERS & LEARNING TO DREAM BIG

REFLECTION & GUIDED SELF-ASSESSMENT QUESTIONS

What are some of your present dreams?

_____
_____
_____
_____
_____
_____
_____
_____
_____
_____
_____
_____
_____
_____
_____
_____
_____
_____
_____
_____
_____
_____

How can you change your environment to promote a mindset that is open to bigger dreams?

What might your bigger dreams look like in the new space of possibility that you have fostered?

LOVING KINDNESS
SHEDDING NEGATIVITY MINDSETS
& EMBRACING OTHERS' DIFFERENCES

Many of us have heard the old phrase "STOP DRINKING THE KOOL-AID!" **Actually**, to defend the good brand name of KOOL-AID, let me make an important distinction; it was actually Flavor Aid that was used in the horrible massacre at Jonestown all those years ago. With greater accuracy, it was pack mentality that caused parents to give their own children a sugary drink laced with poison, before consuming the deadly concoction themselves. Pack mentality is an interesting but fickle thing. At its best pack mentality is key to the preservation of a species; at its worst pack mentality targets minorities and seeks to eradicate free-thought. Pack mentality is responsible for many of the mass tragedies and increased spread of biased propaganda in our world. To be a well-rounded individual; you have to put the Flavor Aid down, and like the few survivors of the Jonestown Massacre, flee into the woods to start looking for your own springs of free thought. Breaking away from the pack is not for the faint of heart, just look at how Scientology and other modern day cults have harmed or completely ostracised people who rejected the tenants of their pack. A former cult member who escapes the pack must be resilient, but also a great strategist willing to risk everything on one chance at the immeasurable and unknown degree of rewarded freedom on the other side.

One of the many non-music jobs that I have had throughout the years included a stint as a substitute teacher in the local public school system. At the time, I was pulled into substitute teaching by former college classmates that were actively pursing careers in K-12 music education. There's a huge deficit between the number of absences and active substitute teachers for general education classes and that number more than triples when one considers the specialised knowledge required to teach art, music, or vocational studies. The direct result of specialist teachers' absences is that there is a break in the curriculum and students, who are already on a tight schedule because of mandated state testing either miss an important unit or are stressed with twice the work in a class that should be a reprieve from the hardened test-based structure of core classes. Having a substitute that is a practicing artist means that the county's public school music teachers can leave a lesson plan behind with the confidence that it will be followed and that their students will be on track for when they return.

I will admit right now that my life was never as full of complaints and overall negativity than when I was texting or conversing with these former classmates turned county music educators. Yes, teaching is a difficult profession. Yes, there is a lot of pressure. Yes, children are much more spirited and perhaps much more disrespectful than in generations past. Yes, there are visible disparities and a general lack of resources for teachers and students alike. However, complaining about a problem without attempting to change it, does nothing but grow an unpleasant grey cloud around one's physical and mental spaces.

The most productive teachers and the happiest teachers that I came across during my tenure as a substitute, weren't necessarily the ones with the most advanced classrooms or the most even-tempered children; rather, these were educators who understood that teaching much like an art form or long-term relationship, requires practice and consistency. These were teachers that entered the classroom with a mindset that was steeped in positivity and informed strategy, acknowledging the tangible struggles that they might face in the classroom, often prepared with an arsenal of solutions and accommodations. These were teachers that had a profound respect for their students, and spoke to them in a manner that prompted the child to think and defend a viewpoint rather than regurgitating things so that the teacher could look good on performance reviews. These were teachers that ran their classrooms in a style that could be paralleled with a form of music that is frequently referred to by modern practitioners as "structured improvisation." While there exist many techniques and methods for structured improvisation the general common thread that binds these disparate ideas under the same umbrella are parameters that can be followed by the ensemble as a large unit and smaller subsections are clearly defined, such that they can be recalled by any member of the group in summary. Structured improvisation is also, a method of controlling chaos, and creating an ad hoc social structure on the fly. When the rules for the improvisation come into play, it clearly begins to address roles and power structures within the group – improvising musical ensembles that have worked together for many years may use hand signals[1] to indicate various on the spot compositional changes or behaviours – in American elementary school classrooms you can often see this power structure in play, when a child needs to go to the bathroom during a lesson and holds up to crossed fingers or three fingers like the letter "W" to replace the need to interrupt a lecture to ask to use the water fountain. When I participated in a larger improvisational ensemble at the Waterloo Region Contemporary Music Sessions in late-summer 2018, we spent several days working on hand signals that would streamline the flow of nonverbal communication necessary for a seemingly flawless performance that was sculpted in real time using our secret coded hand signals. Now removed from that experience, I could easily say that if the group was reassembled with the same performers, we would likely be able to recall our cipher and furthermore, the camaraderie that bound us together in the creation and refinement of hand signals would likely evoke reverie resulting in a seamless efficient flow from rehearsal mode to performance mode.

I made a conscious decision to stop associating with individuals that spent most of their conversation time complaining to me about this or that without brainstorming ways to change their situations. I stopped texting them, I blocked them from my social media accounts, and I deleted their numbers from my phone. Almost immediately, I began to notice a lightening within my own thoughts as heavy negativity energy began to dissipate from my conscious mind. The brightness of positive-thinking also improved my physical health, and the clearing of negative clutter from the corners of my mind, afforded added mental space to really explore new artistic ideas. Negative loops clutter the mind as an insignificant pile of refuse left to grow into a landfill, soon blocks the picturesque view of the scenic mountains or beach that people would formerly pay top dollar to live near; but people generally don't like to live near landfills, and they don't generally like to allow their space to be blacked out by the negative energy of others.

---

[1] A specific example of this is the San Francisco-based Rova Saxophone Quartet. I first became acquainted with their music and use of hand signs through my dear friend, percussionist Justin Greene, while we were working in the aforementioned improvisatory quintet in Waterloo, Ontario in the summer of 2018. While we crafted our own primitive signal language during our week residence in Waterloo, the interested reader can find further information about well-defined use of the Rova Saxophone Quartet's signals in the resource section at the back of this book.

In American schools today, there is a palpable war between clearly defined factions of parents, teachers, school administrators, county administrators, the department of education. The group that suffers largest casualties of this war, are the students who have less than stellar learning experiences because of all the infighting and resentment that happens inside and outside of the classroom. While the most localised example of the "US vs. THEM" mentality is embedded in our community school system, the poisonous phenomenon extends to almost every level of society today – Liberals vs. Conservatives; Democratic vs. Republican; USA vs. EU; and the list continues on… The fundamental problem with "US vs. THEM" mentality is that as each side hardens it's armour for battle, the common good of all people is lost, in a never ending war between sides for whom is irrevocably in the right. There are always going to be people with opposing views; it is healthy and necessary for society to evolve. If we all believed the same things, if we all lived the same way, if we all agreed on every single thing; we might have a surface utopia but it would be bland, lacklustre, and devoid of the improvisation that makes life the vibrant coursing indescribable existence that we feel with each breath.

We dehumanise individuals when we label them. We dehumanise individuals when we lump them in to generalised categories. We dehumanise people when we distill their essence to the observable trends used for data projections and statistics. When we deny someone agency to their individuality, it becomes easier to vilify them or write them off without getting to know what they really think and the nature of their hearts. It is up to us to be open enough to question those with whom we have opposing views; and beyond the surface questions that lead to heated political or religious arguments, we need to delve deeper into how they came to the conclusions that they allow to dictate their actions. Another important consideration, is remembering to approach every conversation with loving kindness and mild mannered civility; heated discussions can be had without the raised voices and name calling that upends the credibility of all sides. People rarely change their values over the course of a single conversation, and seeking to "win" is a foolish approach to difficult discourse. If you firmly believe in something with which a friend, colleague, or family member has a dissenting opinion, the best thing one can do is to demonstrate the positive points of your stance through action and openness to questions about the matter. When a disagreement is met on the battleground of positive action rather than negative rouse, you just may find that your opponent has begun to come around to your way of thinking. On the flip side, you can't always change people's minds, but that doesn't mean that you should approach them with any less loving kindness than those with whom you agree. Loving kindness requires both courage and patience, which are things that we tend to forget about when the basic tasks of life have been automated to eliminate the need to cue for food, or other necessities.

In a generation that grew up knowing "friends" on the other side of the world, where the old adage "don't talk to strangers" has been burned to ash and lost on the wind – how much do you really know about the person next door? The shocking answer, for most individuals is that they know very little about their neighbours and community. At a time when we are so often looking to the other side of the world for chances to dole out kindness through online petitions and fundraisers, there are often people in need at home that are over-looked.

The thing about kindness, is that just like a single acoustic fundamental tone without the benefit of amplification, it is incredibly intense near the source but its effectiveness is lessened the further you move away; however, when a resonant chain reaction is started, the strength of the initial kindness is genuinely felt quite far away. Consider the power of a single violin to effect the SPL or sound pressure levels[2] in a great room, while beautiful playing touches the soul and intelligent design capitalise on the natural resonant reverb of a space; a single violin can in no way smack you in the face as the power of the massive violin sections required to play Wagner or Mahler to their specifications. Kindness resonates in the same manner as sympathetic strings in an

---

[2] While sound pressure levels can be measured scientifically, with various devices; humans are very capable of perceiving intense changes in SPL. Think about the way your ears compress in a very loud environment, or how you can "feel" the kick drum in a small bar with a live band. As a person, who's especially sensitive to sound and vibrational energy; I have always associated high SPL with heat, and no matter how cold a venue is, I immediately feel a rush of heat when the SPL dips into an unsafe realm. Hearing protection becomes incredibly important for those who make a living as performers or engineers or work in other loud environments such as airports or factories, but even the lay person that spends a short amount of time in these environments should take care to protect their hearing by carrying ear plugs with them on a regular basis. Carry ear plugs and hand sanitiser on your person at all times,, turn your headphones down, and watch how impressed your doctors will be at how much your hearing has been preserved over the years!

orchestral section where small concessions for pitch and projection are being made for the greater good of sending one full and unified sound to the back of a massive hall.

I have been incredibly fortunate enough to have lived in the same house for my entire life, bar two years for college in Lakeland. My neighbourhood has evolved a lot over thirty years. The vacant lots that hid all manner of Florida wildlife from creepy snakes to vibrantly coloured yet equally disturbing grasshoppers, have been claimed by man for new houses. A neighbourhood full of young children, soon became one of empty nesters, with occasional renters. The amount of wildlife that frequented my yard from the nearby nature preserve, such as hawks that would perch on our tall white fence whilst scoping out their next meal, are a less frequent sight these days. However, for all the changes, there are still many constants – birds in the oak tree outside my bedroom window chattering day and night, cicadas singing the summer song of their people as something of a natural white noise din, big Florida lizards that creep into the house like a Trojan Horse that I still call my father to come capture, or the frog that apparently thought hanging out in my mum's shower was a cool plan. While the landscape and encounters with nature are a constant story, in the human sector the spirit of community on our block has not been altered over the course of several decades.

In 2017 when Hurricane Irma, a storm that was so powerful it sucked the water out of Tampa Bay, struck our area, we somehow managed to escape unscathed (minus mass power outages that were slow to be rectified by Duke Energy, and lack of Internet service because Spectrum apparently thought running off of Duke's main grid was a sound idea – Yes, I'm throwing shade because this was definitely not Florida's first tango with a massive hurricane, and the state's utility services should have been better prepared.) huge limbs fell from the oak trees outside my house – in fact, massive oak trees near the golf course and nature preserve were ripped right out of the ground, root system and all. One of the first things that you do as a native Floridian, if you have chosen to hunker down and shelter in place in lieu of evacuating, once the storm passes you go outside and assess damage, then you remove any debris that could become problematic in the face of more serious weather. After Irma, one of my uncles came over from his house to help my dad look over the outside of the property. One large limb from an oak tree was near my father's SUV, which is the vehicle that we would have had to use in case we needed to evacuate post-storm for any reason. So here my father and uncle stood, pulling with all their might to get the limb near the street so my other uncle could cart it safely away with his trailer. All of a sudden, the sound of hurried footsteps across tall grass that hadn't been cut due to collective uncertainty of the storm's track and intensity, gave way to the familiar sight of one our next door neighbours, Mr. Mike. He had noticed my family struggling to move the limb, and before we could say anything he jumped in to help, pulling and tugging alongside my dad and uncle, until Mr. Mike got the idea to use one of his saws. He ran back to his place and cut the massive piece of wood into manageable sections, which we then be placed safely by the street for pick up.

Kindness without expectation is something that I remember fondly about growing up on my block. One of my neighbours fought a serious illness that kept her bedridden and weak for a long time, and my dad happily chipped in without her asking for help to keep her lawn mowed during the time she was healing. I went running through my extended neighbourhood one day, and got so caught up with my wind sprints that I didn't realise I had dropped the keys to my house a few streets over, on a particularly fast wind sprint. I got to my house exhausted and disheartened to find that I couldn't get inside to hydrate or take a shower; fully cognisant that because we don't keep a spare key outside the house, I'd be forced to wait in the hot sun for at least thirty minutes until another family member could drive back home. Distraught and anxious, I took a chance to retrace my steps; the moment I rounded the corner where my keys had fallen, my neighbours' gardener ran up to me and returned my keys with a big smile on his face and some kind words to brighten my day.

Let me admit a secret to you dear reader, I have a strange habit of collecting my change and putting it in meters downtown. One day I was leaving a meeting at The Museum of Fine Arts in Saint Petersburg, when I happened upon a woman who parked next to me, visibly flustered, late for work, having great difficulty with finding change to pay the meter; I kindly said, "No worries! This one is on me, and I hope you have a pleasant day at work!" I filled the meter for the maximum time, went my separate way, my only reward a grateful smile and feel of the air as chaotic energy morphed into calming energy the instant that I simply offered to slip some quarters into a meter. A simple seemingly mundane kindness for a stranger I have never seen again is just another example of small acts making the world better. A former student from one of my days as a substitute in a youth diversion program[3] in the county, was my cashier at the hardware store. The young woman immediately recognised me, and though I had trouble placing her in my memory, I could sense that something was bothering her, so I casually asked her how things were going. She proceeded to tell me that she had been taken to task by her manager because a duo of thieves had scammed her with an elaborate gift card setup. She was near tears as she explained that this was her first real job and she really needed to keep it to help her family. I calmly listened to her story, acknowledging the validity of her feelings, and then reminding her that while this one day might have been trying, she had a sea of success ahead of her and now she can move forward with this lesson about suspicious activity to quickly flag and address similar client behaviour in the future. As I finished, speaking with her, I could see a lightness in her eyes and a true belief in the possibilities before her. Loving kindness doesn't require herculean feats of strength or a great deal of extra effort, and it isn't to be repaid in any transactional terms. Seemingly small insignificant incidents in my life, many that happened a year or more ago from the time that I sat down to pen this book, are ease to recall in vivid detail because of how they made me feel and how they changed the emotional course of the individuals on the receiving end of the kindness.

My favourite coffee shop in my hometown of Saint Petersburg, Florida is called Bandit Coffee Co. I have been going to the shop since it first opened. I always say, home never feels completely like home until I've gone to Bandit for coffee and rehearsed on the concert grand piano at The Palladium Theatre. In other chapters, I'll go into more detail about the effects of touring and being a bit of an artistic nomad from the

---

[3] Diversion program is the preferred term for what were previously called "dropout prevention programs" because positive language that removes the assumed label of a "bad kid", has been shown to empower youth to move into a paradigm of positive decision making by teaching them that the nature or value of their worth is not dictated by one single questionable choice, and they have the power to change the direction of the lives for the better.

physical and psychological perspectives, but for now I will touch on the subject of isolation to illustrate how kindness radiates. I go to Bandit for two primary reasons, the first is that they have THE BEST COFFEE, and tied for first is that they have THE BEST PEOPLE at every level of their business. I have had so many conversations with employees, owners, shop regulars, and at the end of the day, I always feel as though I am part of a genuine community. When I come home from being on the road working essentially twenty-four hours a day for at least a two weeks to as much as a month and a half; there's something about being greeted by warm familiar smiles and genuinely being asked about how things are going that pulls me out of my solitude and inspires me to want to interact with the community from which I hail. I actively want to support not just Bandit as a company, but I am invested in supporting the dreams of the employees that work at the shop, many of whom are artists in their own right.

Think about the morning cup of coffee you purchase on an off-day, if someone smiled at you and took a moment to speak to you human-to-human, to acknowledge your feelings and in so doing foster a bright spot that can fundamentally change the trajectory of an otherwise cloudy day – suddenly, you regularly leave the coffee shop with the totally necessary caffeine to power through your day, but you also have a renewed sense of positive energy, which probably radiates into extra patience with frazzled co-workers, and an overall camaraderie between workers that boosts productivity. Now imagine what the world might look like if every company or individual you interacted with showed the loving kindness that everyone at Bandit shows me on a regular basis. How much more positive energy would you have in the day? How would your outlook on the possibilities of your life be altered, simply by replacing negative energy with loving kindness? The positivity and purposeful energy that owners Sarah and Josh Weaver have cultivated with Bandit, and the relationships that I have fostered with other people-centric local businesses owners has a profound effect on my purchasing behaviour on the road; I go out of my way to support local businesses. A prime example was faithfully waking up an hour before everyone else to walk a mile to the local coffee shops in Waterloo, to avoid going to the Starbucks right outside the hotel. By the time I left Waterloo a week later, I had built a solid rapport with the local baristas and was truly sad to part ways. Beyond just supporting these institutions with money, I am fully cognisant that loving kindness can and should extend to the humanity within us all – I make a point to share an extra smile and always seek to make genuine connections with people acknowledging that they are more than the sum of their occupations or struggles.

Some of the most self-described open-minded people I have met are actually the ones who espouse a gospel of Flavor Aid with the strongest vigour. In such situations where there is a large degree of pressure to conform to social "norms," a lot of coat-switching occurs because most people are afraid of going against the pack; and in an effort to conform for fear of retribution, voices are suppressed and people feel a shame that is in direct opposition to the open-minded values that are preached within a social group.

I was raised by a head-strong mother who traveled the world before global women's rights was an initiative, in a world that was a direct opposite to the one in which we presently live. A 5'1" powerhouse who continues to inspire me, she raised me on stories of a world in which she had to overcome numerous hurdles because of her gender. She always raised me to question things. She made everyday tasks such as car rides, groceries, and other mundane chores places for learning by creating space for discussing the intersections of historical events and present day issues. My mother never told me what to think, but always asked me why I thought something had happened in a particular way or how certain people might have come to a particular decision. If I couldn't understand a word or concept, my mum always asked me to isolated the Latin root of the word and to deduce the meaning from there. If I couldn't figure it out from the root, I always had to look up the information for myself, using a dictionary or encyclopaedia, and then summarise the definition in my own words.

It was this upbringing of questioning and the support of coming to my own conclusions that lead me to a controversial turning point in my youth. As a young woman I became steadfast in the concept of feminism as the ability for women to make choices for themselves and to have full agency over their bodies. I have mixed in many different circles, because I think it widens our world view when we get to intimately understand alternate belief structures through the eyes of friends. A large catch of the individuals with whom I have spent time throughout my post-secondary school years would label themselves as bohemians, poets, artists, activists, and counterculture creatives who largely saw a major component of feminism as the full embrace of sexuality through casual lovers, premarital intimacy, and polyamorous encounters. I shied away from ever sharing with people that were very convinced they were my closest friends how uncomfortable their general assertions about my body, about my experience, and about my sexuality made me feel. I never judged them for choosing to have intimate relationships before marriage, but there was always a thick layer of judgement smog the moment that anyone found out that my views on romantic relationships and intimate matters didn't align with theirs. In my humble opinion, if feminism affords a woman the right to choose, and that includes the right to choose to be abstinent, to wait for a serious commitment of a lifetime. In my case, I identify as a cisgender woman, who is open to the possibility of a long-term committed relationship with a cisgender man, who wants to know my mind, heart, and soul first… at the same time, I am incredibly content if I just spend the rest of my days focused completely on my career. To write those words and to speak them today, has been an intense journey filled with shame because I didn't fall in line with the expectations of what a feminist was supposed to be; yet, our minds and bodies and hearts defy expectations all the time.

Feminism is about choice on another level, it doesn't subscribe to the paradigm that you need another individual to validate your existence. A feminist enters a relationship as an independent woman who makes a conscious decision to choose to grow with a particular person. With the agreed upon conjecture that feminism is about choice, does anyone in modern society really have the right to mock a woman who has made a conscious decision to be abstinent, no matter how old they might be?

Condescension and assumption breed shame, which causes people to be less than authentic. Lack of authenticity often leads to repressed negative feelings, and feeds a seeming never-ending loop of negativity.

I don't think that it wrong for any young woman who has thought through her decision with her head and knowledge of her heart to choose to wait for physical intimacy. I do not believe that her choice should be discouraged or treated with shame. I believe that we should celebrate those who have chosen paths of celibacy and abstinence as much as we celebrate those who have chosen their own brand of sexual liberation. I write these incredibly challenging words, because I know that somewhere there is a young woman who is questioning all of this in her mind and feeling pressure from society to go against her gut reactions to wait. She needs to know, that there is nothing wrong with her, and she can hold her head up high knowing that she is not the only one who has come to this decision for herself.

The assumptions about my body, my sexuality, and my experience wore on my heart; the inauthenticity of it all felt like a layer of caked red clay that I could never shed. Just before I turned 28, I felt a welling up of emotion, and a definitive need to finally take back my agency over my body and reputation. I felt as though I was going to implode from holding everything in, while, well-meaning misplaced advised from "woke" women who had been telling me every chance they had that I needed to just "get laid" and "take a lover" because they were "worried" about me being unhappy. I plucked up the courage to meet these ladies separately, and over several cups of coffee explain that I wasn't interested in casual flings or detached physical intimacy. I told them that my personal decision about my body and heart, came not from patriarchal imposed values but rather through deep rumination, self-analysis and critique over the years all leading to the firm belief that engaging in such affairs would personally make me feel hollow and horrible. Furthermore, there are so many things about life that inspire happiness and the pondering of wondrous contentment, I do not feel the exploration of physical intimacy is paramount to feeling fulfilled or passionate about my life. Ironically, many older artists in a variety of mediums have later disclosed to me that their most passionate and involved relationships had a level of stagnation or toxicity that hindered their work… not that I needed any validation in my choices, but I find it interesting to hear how one's artistic practice can be effected either positively or negatively by the intimate relationship in one's life… however, I digress.

If you tell someone you are thirty years old with no physical intimate history of which to speak, the label that becomes attached to you is that of a "Conservative Christian" and therefore must also, side with right wing agenda and is Pro-Life... , etc. It was exactly this set of negative connotations that came with having a different opinion about how I intended to live my own life, that caused me to clam up during many conversations or nervously laugh when the topics turned to bedroom matters. The label of "Conservative Christian" hung over my head like a death nell, particularly in an industry where my choice to be abstinent until I was in a serious committed relationship, that became a potential scarlet letter waiting in the wings to be pinned to my chest and with it the possibility of being blacklisted from various opportunities because of a perceived prudish nature. The labels, of "Conservative Christian" or "assumed liberal" led to me wearing a series of lead masks – nothing good comes from concealing what is in our hearts. Today I stand firm in my refusal to be labeled.

Today I stand firm in my right as a feminist to define myself and to reclaim agency over my body. I believe that everyone has been given freewill and they are the ones who have to live with the results of their decisions. I believe that I alone have the right to judge my actions. I may seek to analyse the thought processes and general logic of the actions of others in a pursuit to understand other individuals' mores and modes of logic, but at the end of the day, it is not my place to project my ethical assessments on anyone but myself. Today, now that my personal truth is out in the open, I feel a weight lifted and I move forward on my purpose driven path with one less bag of unnecessary masks.

Judgement and analysis are two very different mindsets, with contrasting objectives. I have always had a deep fascination with why people make certain choices over others, why certain people believe this over something or someone else – analysis comes from a place of curiosity, while judgement centres on a series of narrowly defined categorisations. It is the variety in our thought processes and experiences that make for a planet full of individuals. While our ancient ancestors had to be constantly weary of differences because pack mentality was key to surviving in a primitive world where dependable shelter from apex predators was scarce; modern humans in organised societies do not have to depend upon single-minded group thought to survive day-to-day, which means they are free to delve into accepting, tolerating, and exploring the specific qualities that make John Smith of Montana in contrast to John Smith who hails from Amsterdam... With the advent of the Internet and ease of global travel, we are in a special time where first hand accounts of cultural traditions and personal thoughts can be explored by anyone with a respectful heart and curious mind. The remarkable result of increased exposure to the diverse world before us, is an exponential increase in the basic questioning of what one knows, while simultaneously cementing certain personal beliefs through virtual as well as physical travel.

Our belief structure is one of the few things in life of which, we can be the master architect. While there is a sea of advice of best practices and popular trends on how to build a house or a concert hall, an architect conducts independent research informed by years of training and experience to put their own spin on the design. Freewill and a marvellous mind capable of all manner of thought, afford us the precious opportunity to design the reality of our beliefs, which are likely to be informed but not defined by exterior sources.

LOVING KINDNESS
SHEDDING NEGATIVITY MINDSETS
& EMBRACING OTHERS' DIFFERENCES

REFLECTION & GUIDED SELF-ASSESSMENT QUESTIONS

Who are the people in your life that consistently bestow acts of loving kindness on you?

_____

_____

_____

_____

_____

_____

_____

_____

_____

_____

_____

_____

_____

_____

_____

_____

_____

_____

_____

_____

_____

_____

_____

What are ways that you could resonate the loving kindness bestowed upon you to others?

What are some simple random acts of kindness that you can incorporate into your everyday life?

What are the topics presently caught in your complaint loop?

How can you change the language you use to describe topics in your complaint loop?

How can you change the circumstances surrounding the issues in your complaint loop?

Who are the negative influencers in your life?

What can you do to expose yourself to belief structures that differ from your own? How can you approach these individuals with a respectful heart and curious mind?

DECAY

FORWARD MOMENTUM
AVOID GETTING STUCK IN THE PAST-POSITIVE AND PAST-NEGATIVE

YOUR LIFE AND YOUR CAREER ARE NOT WIND SPRINTS, rather they are a marathon where energy conservation is critical to longevity and overall performance. People often talk about the crucial need to move past your negative experiences so that you can embrace a new positive future; few people talk about how big movements and positive feelings associated with successes can turn into quick sand.

The day before my large concert at St. Petersburg College, my piano professor Jeff Donovick imparted the wisdom that the next twenty-four hours marked a "big moment" for me, but that this was just one of many "big moments." It is this advice that has carried me through the fast-paced career of a working artist. Many artists struggle with the tremendous amount of pressure that comes from being required to perform at a high-level with consistency. Stage fright and fear of public speaking are also things that many people struggle to manage, but the thing is once you change the internal narrative – once you realise that that big meeting, that huge client, that large public exhibition, is just one of many across a lifetime of success on your purpose path; the build up of emotion and anxiety that comes with placing all your eggs in one basket dissipates considerably. I am incredibly lucky that I have never had to fight with stage fright in my professional career, and rather I feel the most at home on stage or in front of an audience; but I have coached many artists and entrepreneurs across several disciplines and all of them have stated that the moment they embrace changing the narrative in their minds they become more confident in their negotiations and public presentations.

Some people live in the victories of the past without knowing how to move forward and embrace the present situation before their eyes. We are familiar with the cautionary tale of the jock who "peaked" in high school only to become a raging alcohol who sits in his easy chair at home, surrounded by squaller, pushing back beer after beer; watching a football game and rambling incoherently about how he could have been one of the players on the field if it hadn't been for this or that reason. This trope is the extreme, but how many of us are guilty of continuing the mental celebration party past midnight? My father has always said, "Nothing good happens after midnight." and though he was specifically referencing the physical dangers of the night, the same adage holds true for partying in your emotions past a reasonable time. Yes, you should certainly pat yourself on the back for a job well done, but resting your laurels on a single success or catch of successes is like running on a treadmill – sure you increase your endurance, but ultimately you are left in the same place that you started. When you approach successes and failures as hurdles on a dynamic track or perhaps even an epic parkour run, you can easily mark how many kilometres you have traveled because the scenery has changed significantly.

My dear piano professor, Jeff Donovick, who's lessons weren't entered sole on the piano but rather took a wholistic approach which prepared me to fully evolve into the mindset of a professional artist; often said, "Most people change their molecules every seven years. Elizabeth changes her molecules every seven months." A truer statement could not be made about how I view myself as person and as an artist, I firmly believe to get to the next level we have to moult our old molecular shells an embraces the nest stage of metamorphosis.

As a trained audio engineer, I am the one that friends and colleagues seek out for opinions on recordings, for mixing and tracking work, as well as for adjudication in calls for submissions. The exposure of a wide variety of projects throughout my year results in a strong sonic understanding of trends in the musical world in both the academic sector and the public sector. I have done deep listening on many of music compositions rising stars from the days that they were in school and I can easily pick their works out of a blindfolded lineup because they rely heavily on a "signature" style. People think that when you find a path to success, when you find the formula that keeps winning you prize after prize, you should continue down that path and rubric. When we rest our laurels on formulaic creation, signature styles, and uninterrupted routines we become akin to an old statute in the centre of a busy city park that becomes increasingly ignored as people become desensitised to the features that once were the literal "talk of the town."

"Falling in line" was the expectation of industrial era society, but as we move forward into a new world order where eclecticism and innovation are consistently chosen over the path well-trodden, we have to think about ourselves, our creative output, and our relationships in an entire new manner. Resting on one's laurels leads to resentment and contempt, these are to fundamental reasons that couples and indeed employees often choose to break away from their partners or companies. There is a living aspect to art and neglecting to shake up your relationship with your craft, will often result in getting stuck in a rut whereby one continues churning out the same material under different names.

When I look at my friends with steadfast marriages or partnerships, they are without a doubt, the relationships where I can clearly chart how the choice to bind themselves to another human pushed them to evolve as artists and as individuals, because within the unit both people wanted to see the other succeed and were willing to mutually make concessions and work together to become more well-rounded people. My relationship with my art has followed the lead of a successful relationship, because not only do I consistently spend time trying to get to know more about my chosen mediums, we also explore new ideals together in my conceptual works that probe into philosophy, physics, and metaphysics. Perhaps most importantly, I take the time to notice how my art evolves week to week and year to year, how my touch on the piano or phrasing of a particular section evolves in various works over time.

I will never purport to be perfect, and my twenties were in many ways, full of lessons about resting on various triumphs. After every large scale professional success, I often found myself yearning for a measure of "normal" personal success (long-term relationships etc.) and in my quest for meaningful relationships with others, I didn't purse my professional career with as much vigour as I should have and could have because I had distracted myself with going out to concerts and hanging out with people, who it turned out were more preoccupied with my status as an artist and what they could gain from an association with me, rather than an actual personal interest in getting to know me and my heart.

I believe that we are called to assist others in need, no matter how inconvenient it might be or how pressing the hour. My college path was a winding and unexpected journey; while still in high school I began taking classes at the local community college, which was just down the street from the catholic high school that I attended. I suppose this was the universe's nod toward my middle school experience, where I took advanced math classes at the high school while still enrolled at my catholic feeder school.

It was the early days of social media and everyone had their own myspace, people we spending hours on the web talking to people, thinking that we truly knew their hearts and souls. As part of my undergraduate requirements for a degree in music, I was forced to take College Choir because I was a classical guitar performance major, my ensemble options were limited until I transferred to Florida Southern College where I was afforded the chance to take Guitar Ensemble because I was able to play with my teachers as a trio.

While attending the community college choir, I befriended a young woman named Lilith who had been homeschooled for most of her life, and purported to have restrictive and otherwise abusive parents. I began to speak to her via Myspace chat regularly and even collaborated with her on a couple of fledgling music projects. Our friendship seemed deep and true and genuine… and on Lilith's eighteenth birthday, when she called me in tears proclaiming between sobs that her parents had thrown her out on the street; without hesitation, my family stepped in near midnight to collect her and the belongings that her parents had tossed into garbage bags on the front lawn amidst flashes of blue and red police lights – that evening we took her into our home without question. My parents treated Lilith as their own, helping her transition into adulthood from working to setup an apartment of her own, assisting with getting her first car, and counselling her on how to become financially stable. Even though she later moved in with a boyfriend, she still spent many evenings sleeping over at my house, having dinner prepared by my mum and receiving the support of a loving family.

Appearances are not always what they seem to be, and in truth Lilith was bleeding my parents financially, and causing a huge rift between me and my family. My cousins were upset that I had chosen to continue to support a stranger over my parents wishes to cut her off. In my own heart, I was having a stream of doubts about the genuine nature of our friendship. Lilith was obsessed with men and her looks, spending hours on the phone every day flirting with this or that guy. I remember being inwardly frustrated when I wanted to have a meaningful conversation and she would compulsively look at her phone. Perhaps, this is the reason why today I have issues with people that constantly check their phone and avoid eye contact with me during a serious conversation. The rift evolved into a slow growing supernova, which then collapsed into a black-hole, in the wake of my twenty-first birthday.

A few days before my twenty-first birthday, I went to pick Lilith up from her job at a retail store at the local mall. I remember well, that my parents had entered into a serious argument about how much time the Lilith was spending at the house without contributing to the household. I took the highway in my old Mercedes-Benz, my first car, a beautifully restored 1991 190E, an unexpected Christmas gift from my parents just a few short years before. I clearly remember the song that was an repeat before I pulled up to the back of the mall to collect Lilith – *A Wolf Sheep's Clothing* by the indie rock band This Providence, when I listen to the lyrics I'm immediately transported back to that night and realise how many of the lines in the actual foreshadowed what would one of the first major betrayals of my life.

All seemed to be calm and regular… I stopped at the intersection just down the road from her retail job as I had done a hundred times before and after she got a car… then out of nowhere it happened – I was rear-ended on the driver's side at full speed by a reinforced air conditioning repair truck going at least 45 mph. The truck backed up out of my mangled trunk and proceeded over the median for a not so clean get away, largely because the name of the company was clearly plastered on the side of the truck. Thankfully, I had an old car made of steel, which saved my life – believe it or not, I was able to drive away from the accident scene. However, I spent the evening in the hospital due to issues with high blood pressure…

On my actual twenty-first birthday celebration at home that Sunday, my mum prepared a special meal, with only one request, that both of us girls set the kitchen table for family dinner together. I remember well the pain I felt, when Lilith, whom I had taken into my home in the middle of the night barely two years before, sat at the table – refusing to help and instead flirting with several men over text. I remember vividly the pain I felt when Lilith had to be coaxed to wish me a "happy birthday" on August 10, 2009, when I had to spend the entire day with her in doctor's office after doctor's office because I had sustained all the injuries from the accident.

The straw that broke the camel's back? When I removed Lilith from my top friends on Myspace. This sent her on a war path to destroy my reputation and friendships at home, while I was away at school. She spent her evenings and work breaks texting the most vile things to me, until I had to call the Polk County Sheriff in the middle of the night for guidance. A formal complaint was filed. The Polk County Sheriff's department issued an order stating that she was not to come in contact with me or they would act swiftly to neutralise any threat she could pose towards me… and I had to change my phone number.

All of this turmoil happened on the cusp of my final solo recital at Florida Southern College. I was physically in a tremendous amount of pain from the spinal injury sustained during the car accident; and I felt a persistent depression from the verbal abuse and systematic destruction of my reputation that I was being subjected to from Lilith back at home; the isolation that I felt within the music department; an immense amount of pressure from my primary guitar teacher who was determined to turn me into his protégée; and a general lack of true support system and camaraderie. For my last semester at Florida Southern College, I woke up every morning to the concrete wall of my dorm room and sobbed hopelessly into my pillow before I got out of bed, because the happiness and comfort I had felt in my reoccurring piano performance dream was far from the dark reality that was thrust upon me forcefully with each sunrise.

There are people that the universe places in your life at just the right moment to help you through times of trouble, and one never knows who the lighthouses in the fog and reduced visibility will be until you go through troubling times. I am a huge proponent of self-motivation and pulling yourself up by your bootstraps to make things happen.

Simultaneously, I accept and acknowledge that sometimes we need people that we trust, the small number of folks who are intimately acquainted with the trials and tribulations on our path to success, the people that often believe in the largeness of our success before we see it in ourselves. In my case, that person is my dear friend Andraya. the person who listened to all my electronic music tracks, who encouraged me to cut ties with people that were just hanging on to my coattails, the person who taught me about graphic design and branding, the person who always found a way to make me laugh through tears; and the person today, who fully understands every ounce of pain that I worked through on my way to what seems to present casual onlookers as smooth sailing on a sea of success.

I was in a place where I was about to graduate from school with a degree in classical guitar performance, and though my final recital was a rough experience; I should have felt the forward momentum of the achievement pushing me into my next endeavour. Instead, I felt incredibly lost, preoccupied by a concert that felt like a complete failure in my perfectionist eyes, on the verge of having to figure out what one actually could do with a degree in classical guitar performance outside of getting a masters degree in classical guitar performance and accruing more debt from student loans without a viable end in sight to pay it back.

Having a person in your life who allows you the space and freedom to bounce ideas around without judgement, while still maintaining a level of realness that causes you to question and probe deeper into your theoretical ideas; is the greatest gift that the universe can afford a living conscious being. That person can come in many shapes and sizes, but that confidant is the definition of a true friend. In a world where we share so much online, and often relate closeness to the quantity of contact instead of the quality of contact; it is interesting to note how many foolish situations arise when one takes the advice of the person that they talk to on a surface level with extreme frequency, over the person who knows them on a deep level with all of the context necessary when considering profound matters. Over many dorm room conversations and 3:00am trips to Walmart to people watch[4] because there was literally nothing to do in Lakeland in those days – I began to gain some semblance of clarity.

Andraya was the one to point out that I had a special ability, to speak the language of both sides of the recording studio glass. I had the traditional training of in classical music school from my studies at Florida Southern College, but during summers I went back to St. Petersburg College and took the music technology courses of the fledgling Music Industry & Recording Arts program to which my ground-breaking "SPC Rocks concert" had given some forward momentum. The more I bounced ideas off of Andraya and the more feedback she gave me, the more apparent it became that I needed to go back to SPC and treat the community college as an experimental ground for developing a brand and artistic voice that could take me into a professional career.

Moving back to my hometown after Florida Southern College was a difficult adjustment in many ways – life doesn't just stop in a place because you go somewhere else, and power structures are constantly changing and shifting over time. I took to the Internet to get to know the new people who had come in to my hometown to wave the flag for experimental and noise music. I met the self-professed king of experimental music in the area Judas. I remember that everyone wanted to be his friend and everyone wanted to be on the shows that he booked. I fell into a peanut butter and jelly pattern with him, conversing every day, working on projects together, taking classes at the community college together, spending time with his girlfriend Crystal. For two years, I felt as if I had a brother that I could always count on to be there. I felt part of a unit. I didn't see that Judas was manipulating me at every turn. I didn't expect that he was saying unkind things about me behind my back. When I refused to accept his new girlfriend, Gemma, after I strung together a sea of lies that she was telling about herself, and when I expressed my opinion that someone who lived his rogue lifestyle of partying, drugs, and unregistered

---

[4] If you every want to do some quality people watching, and shady narration of the very strange behaviours people exhibit when they think nobody is watching – I highly encourage you to head over to your local small town Walmart in the middle of the night and just take a gander at what is probably Netflix's next award-winning production.

firearms was unfit to take on the role of partner and father for a woman with a prepubescent child barely a week after meeting. It was when a woman chose to go against Judas and speak her mind and form her own opinions on a situation; thus challenging his perceived control and authority. I vividly remember sitting on my front stoop the night after my first solo album release show, fielding a call in which he laid into me, calling me every vile and demeaning term that could be thrown at a woman. I was devastated. I was betrayed. I had rely on all the strength of my ancestors to avoid giving him the satisfaction of my tears. I tried to go on living normally, but Judas systematically arranged for me to be followed, and for people to listen in on my conversations. This stranger who had waltzed into my town only a few short years before, was suddenly controlling my reality and threatening my basic comfort in my hometown. I couldn't go to my favourite cafe to have a bite to eat or complain to a local friend about the difficulty and isolation I was feeling without it getting back to him. He had me followed, he had people write harassing messages to me online, he maligned my name with people that I thought were friends, he turned my existence in my hometown into a veritable prison.

At this point, I was faced with a clear and defined fork in the road. I could have easily let my harasser win. I could have easily allowed Judas to keep me cloistered behind the walls of Alcatraz while my body broke down from lack of sunlight and my mind turned to putty from the isolation of solitary confinement; instead I decided that if I was going to be alone, if I was going to exist in a prison-like paradigm where I could only trust myself, I would seek to escape the only way I knew how, I would revert to my primordial form of expression – my first instrument, the piano. For two and a half years, I committed myself to obsessive practice piano and composition. I came to school to practice on the grand pianos before classes began, I practiced in between classes, and I practiced until the security guards had to lock the building for the evening. I took a position as house manager of the music performance hall on campus, so that I could practice on the fine concert grands after concerts. My whole life became about the piano and the comfort of free expression in the safety of my practice spaces. I acquainted myself with the texts of Abby Whiteside and asked Jeff to incorporate more Alexander Technique in my private lessons. I became an astute listener, spending countless hours on honing my touch and growing the shades of my dynamic range. I emerged from this cocoon of focused practice space and time, a burgeoning professional ready to take on a music world that extended far beyond the boundaries of Pinellas County.

Sometimes, our forward momentum is the product of a collaborative effort, and other times a fire within our core grows from smouldering embers into a raging blaze that takes us to new heights. When I walked into the practice room, when I first began to lean on the sonorities that pulled me out of the clutches of a mentally abusive individual that only sought to control me – I had no idea how I would evolve over the course of secluded hours to emerge with the confidence in my abilities and courage of conviction necessary to pursue my career at a level that stretched beyond my wildest dreams.

When it comes to the energy sucking and negative individuals in my past, I look upon them now with kindness and gratitude. I rarely speak their names, because in rehashing each situation it becomes easy to get lost in a loop of negativity. The ancient Egyptians had a habit of erasing the names of people who committed crimes or were otherwise ostracised for attempting to bring harm to the community. You have the power to strike the names of individuals that have meant to cause you harm from the records of your mind, this doesn't mean you forget the lessons that you learned from interacting with someone who sought to feed off of your life-force and your career energy. When you release the names of betrayers and offenders from your memory, you release the power that they hold over you and you create space for new positive growth in the once embittered darkened areas with scar tissue.

Many years removed from these hardships, I have seen several of the individuals that sought to make my existence a prison cell, and I have always felt overcome with an overwhelming sense of gratitude because they strengthened my intestinal fortitude, ultimately inspiring me to believe in a vision of myself and my career that reached outside the local dive bars and unorganised four hour noise shows of experimental works that existed without context or purpose – that in many cases were and still are unsafe exclusionary to women and minorities.

FORWARD MOMENTUM
AVOID GETTING STUCK IN THE PAST-POSITIVE AND PAST-NEGATIVE

REFLECTION & GUIDED SELF-ASSESSMENT QUESTIONS

Think of some people in your life that know "the whole story." The people with whom you can bounce your ideas around, and the ones that will call your bluff. Take some time to list them here, and then take a moment to write a heartfelt letter to each one acknowledging how they have helped you grow as a person.

_____
_____
_____
_____
_____
_____
_____
_____
_____
_____
_____
_____
_____
_____
_____
_____
_____
_____

What are the positive achievements that you tend to rest your laurels upon? How can you shake up your tendencies to propel forward momentum that leaves you open to explore new directions and depths within yourself?

What are the trying moments and energy sucking people that are hindering your forward momentum? Take some time to list them below, and then begin to release their negative hold on you.

FINDING SOLACE IN THE FLOW OF WORK
USING TROUBLING MOMENTS TO REFOCUS
ON GOALS & RESET OBJECTIVES

Old habits are difficult to break, and humans persistently seek some sort of comfort in social interactions. The well-hewn artist that had developed in the practice room, that was then able to carry the torch to the various branches of college bureaucracy to make Elizabeth A. Baker - Solo Piano Compositions in Recital a reality; was out of touch with the customs and relationships of a "normal" twenty-something. I recall one day a guy came by the small recital hall where I regularly rehearsed, he espoused to be sad to have missed my solo piano performance in one of our shared classes, and so I did the most natural thing – I played the piano. Something extraordinary has always happened when I perform, particularly when I am on top of my game; no matter how big or small the audience is, everything melts away and I am drawn into another world where it is only me and my instruments… my sounds, a world that I simply open a portal to for others to look inside. Without a doubt, this is the only place in my whole existence where I have felt completely at home, at rest, and surrounded by something akin to unconditional love.

As the final pitch became one with the natural noise floor of the room and disappeared into the ether of the subconscious, I looked up to find two mesmerised eyes fixed squarely upon me. From that day, I had a new friend, and perhaps a new chap to fancy. My concert preparations finished, I was in a place where I should have been researching and preparing for the next opportunity, for the next lateral move to "level up" my career. Instead, I found my way into an indie rock band and electronic duo with Peter, the fellow that had sat in a lonely recital hall listening to my solo piano practice. I wasted a lot of my brain power, trying to analyse Peter's actions, he would frequently text me some of the sweetest things, and always catch me after practices to talk in front of my car under the soft yellow glow of street lamps… I know what you are thinking dear reader. I know what I thought at the time. I thought that he was warming up to something more than just a platonic friendship; however, there are people in life that think that they know what is best for you, people that interfere with the flow of things, the unknown variables in a physics equation that lead to results that you could have never predicted.

It should have been an exciting night. It was the end of the semester. It was a time for celebration. The band's bass player, Brock was none too happy about the closeness that I'd had formed with the group's drummer, Peter. In his opinion, the drummer needed to make mistakes and grow up before he could appreciate a woman like me, and with this sentiment and these misplaced intentions, one of the hardest nights of my life began. I heard Brock talking to a young woman named Katrina, who had just graduated high school and was looking to explore the adult world. I heard him taking to the Peter trying to push the Katrina and Peter together… I remember the Marion, the lead singer of the band trying to console me in an empty bedroom as I cried tears inspired not only by the hurt of someone I had fancied rejecting me for another female but also, by the deep betrayal that I felt from Brock who had broken the unspoken bond of camaraderie and trust that are necessary to cement any band together. I remember emerging from the empty bedroom to see the Katrina's shoes in front of the Peter's bedroom. I remember just wanting to get out of that house of horrors. I remember driving home through tears with Andraya on speakerphone, worried about me. I remember rock bottom in glimpses of consciousness, the Keirsten coming to visit, the Marion sitting at the foot of my bed, daily calls from Andraya… and the final betrayal, being kicked out of the band by Peter and lectured about how I needed to change, how I was in the wrong for reading into his actions, how I was being an "emotional woman."

Isolation, an all too familiar trope in my life, felt heavy and constricting again. However this time I my coping skills were better informed, I knew the place that I could heal, I knew the place that I could find myself again – the piano, the music, the sonic world. When I entered the practice room this time, I was not going to emerge until I was on my way to an international career. Jeff Donovick, my dear piano professor, offered solace in amusing tropes such as "Pulitzer Prize winners don't have friends." I'm fairly sure that Jennifer Higdon and Kendrick Lamar have friends, but it was the reassurance that I needed to hear at a time when isolation was my norm and socialisation seemed like an insurmountable anxiety inducing task.

One of the hardest working musicians at the college and in the local community is Dr. David Manson, a man that most students write off as a hard teacher. In truth, David Manson is and would be one of my greatest supporters throughout my musical journey. I learned many years earlier during my first stint at St. Petersburg College that David had high standards; his credentials as an artist and arts advocate definitely gave him the clout to back up his pursuit of excellence. David does not throw praise around loosely and to earn his respect is a true honour. One day I was practicing in a classroom down the hall from his private studio, when I received a casual compliment from him about how he had noticed an improvement in my piano playing. It was my dedication to my craft that David saw and heard for several years, and these were values that he supported whole-heartedly. I began to seek out his advice about establishing a career as a touring artist and pursing a nonprofit. To this day I remember one particular conversation with David that changed my career objectives and my approach to my practice profoundly. I came into David's office on an off day for me, I was growing frustrated because I was having issues booking gigs in the area that weren't in bars or places where people gathered less for the music and more for drinking and socialising. Instead of placating me with platitudes about booking being a difficult task, on this day David told me he did not see me making a local career or even a national career, in his own words "[Elizabeth] you are meant to be an international artist."

From that moment, my perception of how I approached my art changed. I completely refused to play in bars. I stopped performing on keyboards because I noticed how weighted keyboards and actually grand pianos are entirely different instruments, requiring different touches and techniques – time spent on keyboards ruined my honed sensitivities and control on a concert grand piano creating a cycle where hours of practice progress gained were subverted by mere minutes of regular hip-hop ensemble rehearsal. I committed to learning all that I could about using Pro Tools[5] as a performative element, spending a good amount of time with Dave Greenberg during his office hours talking about Alvin Lucier and John Cage. When Dave Greenberg, my music technology and mixing professor, encouraged me, with approval from Dr. Jonathan Steele, the Dean of Fine Arts and Music for SPC, to do a my first prepared piano recording; I reluctantly hopped at the opportunity for extended time in the studio and recorded several improvisations with various preparations. It was also, through experiments within Pro Tools that Dave and I worked together to create a template to recreate the iterated reverb effect of Lucier's iconic work *I am sitting in a room (1969)*, which I then warped and modified for my own compositions. The resultant work was *Three Compositions for Piano & Electronics (2013)* one of my first works to be feature on Composer's Circle, and then to go on to receive national attention. Since 2013 when I crafted *Three Compositions* as part of a demo for my capstone project, it has been accepted into festivals, featured on blogs, performed throughout the world as far as China, and been interpreted by pianists' hands beyond my own. Later, I figured out how to code a similar effects chain in Max[6], growing and evolving from that initial understanding of iterated reverb.

Repetition is a surefire way to learn, and sometimes the repetitive lessons comes in the form of mistakes. It was shortly after the success of *Three Compositions* and me beginning to book gigs as far away as Seattle, that I found myself fancying another bloke at school. On the surface he checked most of the boxes, a working artist with regular gigs in local bars, carried around a Moleskine notebook for lyrics and ideas, appeared well-read and generally able to keep up with me in conversation.

---

[5] Pro Tools is the worldwide industry standard software for recording. My history with Pro Tools software accounts for just over a third of my entire life, and I have truly grown up with the program. Even though most people think of Pro Tools as a software program solely for music production, I realised early in my performance career that it was useful as an instrument and a live effects processor.

[6] Max is another common industry program, though from my experience it pops up in the workflow of more academics than it does in the traditional recording studio. Max is a visual programming environment, which makes it conducive to digital media artists as well as sonic artists for interactive performances and increased finesse over parameters that one can't access within Pro Tools, Logic, or other digital audio workstations. I use a lot of different programs to create, and look at each one as a different tool in a box – one wouldn't use a hammer to drill a hole, and one wouldn't use Pro Tools for mapping visuals or the body for reactive purposes.

How often do we ignore red flags because we are blinded by rose-tinted glasses? My mum raised me on old British adage, "A gentleman's word is his bond." And so I trusted that when this young gent, Edison said that he was going to come over to hang out and play music with me, that he would do just that. Hours began to tick by and the Sun dipped below the horizon, direct calls when unanswered, I was so frustrated I went out for a run, finally as I reached the regular turnaround point of my outdoor runs I called his roommate Jeremy to ask what was going on. I never got a straight answer. I did continue to spend time with Edison at his various bar gigs as I had become great friends with his roommate Jeremy who was in several bands with Edison, and the other Ruben worked as a recording engineer (and though he would later break up with her in the worst way, introduced me to another one of my dear friends an accomplished geologist named Nikki McShane). For over a year, I dealt with what I would later come to find out was a type of psychological manipulation and abuse that is now referred to as *gaslighting*[7] – I was consistently made to believe that the world was other than how I saw it, but I had witnesses, friends who stood there while Edison told me that he wanted to spend time with me, and even wanted to have just one day a week to see me, which are all things that he would later deny ever saying and of course refuse to answer the phone. The situation was a precarious one because Jeremy not only played in a band with him, but also worked as a freelance audio engineer for me as a solo artist and later for my nonprofit organisation.

My life is full of awkward and hilarious stories, that I couldn't make up even if I wanted to try and I promise you will find more of them in the following pages of this book, but this one is perhaps up there on the list of things I wish I could un-see or un-experience. One crisp morning, I went to the college early to practice piano as usual, taking a short break to tap out a text Jeremy who had a copy of my session files on an external hard drive that we exchanged about once a week, so I could back up and edit things on my own computer, about getting my external hard drive back that day because there was something on the

---

[7] Gaslighting is a relatively new term, used to describe a sort of mental abuse in which the abuser plants seeds of doubt in the mind of a victim and through continued manipulation, the victim begins to seriously question their perception of reality as well as their ability to recall things from memory.

drive that I wanted to submit to a festival for programming consideration. Jeremy told me that his roommate Edison had it and that the rogue bloke was on campus in the large studio. I knocked on the studio door and politely asked Edison for the drive, the bloke claimed it was at home and that he would give it to me after his class finished later that morning. As was an all too familiar norm, I waited outside the studio for Edison to come out of class only to learn that he had proceeded another way, and when I texted him about meeting up in the parking lot to get my drive from him he claimed that he was going to be busy and unavailable. So I texted Ruben to ask if I could come by and pick up the drive that was allegedly still in their house. Ruben told me to come on by and we could look for the drive together. I arrived at the house and it was then that Ruben and I realised that the hard drive had been in Edison's van the whole time... the only problem is that by now this repugnant lad had been at home in the bathroom with a certain magazine with beautiful women, and just as I turned to leave the awkward situation that was unfolding, the heavens opened up and torrential rain accompanied by violent thunder came out of nowhere essentially trapping me in the house while the Edison finished his magazine inspired business in the loo. Without an umbrella for escape, I sat in the living room with Ruben in uncomfortable silence, wanting to disappear and thankful when one of the cats, Mr. Pickles, curled up on my lap to help ease my anxiety. Yes, boys and girls, I had to wait for my hard drive while this guy finished masturbating. When I got my hard drive back, I don't think that my feet could have carried me fast enough out of there or had a subsequent shower hot enough to wash the gross feelings of lies.

The thing about humans is that we are surprisingly resilient, this would not be my last encounter with Edison. Rather our final standoff would be under dim street light, with the swirling booms as a sea of clubs and bars spewed their sonic pollution into the darkened streets of Ybor City. It was here, under a lamppost that I still pass to this day with vivid flashbacks of the confrontation... yelling, his yelling, and reducing my being to nothing more than that of a "silly woman." I think it is interesting that in break ups and conflicts between men and women there is always an imbalanced expectation that the woman is supposed to "learn a lesson." Edison's final parting words to me were "I hope that you have learned a lesson." They stung, like the tears I tried to hide as they welled up warm and replete with salt that burned my eyes and a rebuttal that stuck in my throat, choking me as it failed to materialise in the night air... today, the microaggression[8] of his words still infuriate me on principle, because in implying that someone ought to learn a lesson, you are denying them agency to their feelings, you are denying any culpability in your role in the situation. When I break down that situation multiple times, I now realise that perhaps I could have been less optimistic and forgiving with my feelings; but I passionately argue that closing ourselves off from the ability to access our emotions on a deep level does nothing to further our growth as beings or artists, and I fundamentally argue that when a person who makes clear promises only to break them, then tries to systematically twist the perception of another human being's reality to fit their destructive narrative – we are talking about mental abuse. We are talking about a paradigm that living in for just over a year, made me doubt my daily perceptions of reality and people's basic intentions for over two years. We are talking about abuse that literally made me feel on the personal side of life, like a failure who was inherently incapable of interacting with other humans on any meaningful level. For two and a half years, I thought that every single compliment that I was ever given was an illusion. For two and a half years, I avoided looking at myself in a mirror. Even the empowered and independent woman that stands before you today, has internal scar tissue in the healing process and an occasional need to push Edison's judgements about her body out of her consciousness, and remind herself that she is indeed a loveable desirable being.

The thing about great pain and turmoil is that it leads to great art. I sometimes question whether, I stayed in such a destructive situation longer than necessary because of the seemingly inescapable trap of mental abuse or the powerful art that I was churning out at the time. Much of my early work, while informed by various philosophical musings was largely influenced by love and the failed pursuit of love in my personal life. After I "learned my lesson," my work began to take on different preoccupations. First, I fell into neuroscience to rationalise the feelings of love and bonding, and found a deep comfort from studying something outside my artistic medium of sound, then subsequent

---

[8] Microaggression is an umbrella term to encapsulate the everyday verbal and nonverbal slights and insults that people dole out intentionally or unintentionally to ostracise others and otherwise breed hostility within an environment.

process of attempting to synthesise my experience or understanding of the material into a tangible sonic works. Today, while I think of my mature body of work from conceptual viewpoints, my heart and soul personality still resonate from a pure centre that has somehow still maintained its hopeful curiosity and belief in the goodness of humankind.

Artists have sometimes been referred to as latent masochists, because we thrive on the inspiration born in moments of pain and strife; however, this preoccupation is an unhealthy one. If you dwell in the land of lows for a prolonged period of time you are destined to feel as though you have fallen into a bottomless void, from which there is no means of escape. The difficulty with being a natural-born artist, is that you are constantly experiencing emotions at a deeper base-level than many others, from a metaphysical perspective this is often explained by the assertion that highly sensitive artists are natural empaths. When you sit in the darkness of troubling experiences, leaving a paper trail into the light – as you traverse further into the depths of black, the light grows dim, your paper trail of achievements and work become increasingly difficult to distinguish from the expanding void around you – this is clinical depression, this is when basic tasks become akin to climbing Mount Everest, this is performing a killer show only to return home to feelings of disconnection, this is the what hides behind the face of people with high-functioning depression, this is what leads to self-medicating, and ultimately, if left unaddressed… this is what leads to untimely death.

I am not a licensed mental health professional, but I have firsthand experience in the realm of dealing with mental health on one's own, the benefits of speaking up and getting the help that one needs to feel better and operate at their optimum potential. I have lost many friends and colleagues to suicide when they did not reach out and get the help they needed, because we as a society and particularly as an arts industry association any "fault" whether physical or mental as the basis for immediate exile and isolation. A global tendency to label individuals with mental health issues as a defective, and further dehumanise them by using their medical conditions as source for comedic fodder. The truth is that if we were more open and frank about our struggles with mental health, we would happen upon a network of people with similar struggles to embrace us, instead of concealing our wounds in shame for the sake of assimilation into an ableist world. You know what happens to an untreated wound? It festers, turns gangrenous until intervention causes you to lose that body part. If the infected wound is left completely untreated, you pay the ultimate price with your life. Mental health is an unseen wound, and like many "invisible illnesses" we want to deny that it exists and we fail to acknowledge that itchy fall into the category of a disability.

The orchestra player that has tinnitus because of the modern obsession with making ensembles louder, hides their invisible illness because they are convinced that disclosure of it will cause them to lose their jobs and status. The person with anxiety often drinks at music events to ease the stress of dealing with other humans in an enclosed space, they are the life of the party… until they are not… until they drink too much. The composer with bipolar disorder who enters rehearsal seemingly "off" but is forced to push through rather than being afforded the time to reset through self-care techniques recommended by a licensed medical professional, is given the titles of eccentric and difficult to work with – a reputation that trickles through the gossip channels until that person sees a marked reduction in commissions and the ability to pay for critical medical care. We could easily rectify these situations, the orchestral player can receive regular care from a specialist, we can create more intimate spaces and opportunities for performances, we can create a crisis network, we can rearrange schedules… but ultimately, change has to occur in three places – first, those living with invisible illnesses have to speak up; second, we need to create safe spaces for people to speak up; third, we need to figure out reasonable accommodations and support networks to handle these issues. On an organisational level, we are discussing the creation and implementation of programs. On the individual level this means, looking outside of ourselves and embracing those around us, employing the loving kindness we discussed in a previous chapter.

Focusing on my artistic practice and projects are two of the most effective ways for me to personally combat depressive thoughts, there's no universal recipe for combating the very natural lows that we experience as humans – but my inward motto has always been "Don't get mad. Get to work. Don't live in sad. Get to work." The comfort of work is that there is always more to do, and as an artist more to explore and learn. For people who are in other sectors of the economy "get to work" can be translated to "get to work on yourself." When an artist delves into their practice with fervour, forsaking the paradigms that have sought to destroy them from the inside out; one has to embrace an examination of the self and the world around them. When I was told that I needed to "learn my lesson," I wanted to know why I had been attracted to such a destructive individual in the first place. When my former classmates tried to take apart my life brick by brick, I want to know why some humans feel such an extreme and immediate bond with each other, and why people are more apt to save their most striking betrayal for those with whom they formerly shared a seemingly close relationship. All of these questions, brought me in to the cursory study of neuroscience and the structures of the chemical compounds that influence so many of our feelings without conscious attention. While I didn't set out to reset the objectives of my work, the fundamental wish to explore why things were happening – to understand the things below the surface resonated into a body of works that have been praised by critics, academics, and the public for their genuine pure-hearted exploration of complex issues in fields outside of the arts.

FINDING SOLACE IN THE FLOW OF WORK
USING TROUBLING MOMENTS TO REFOCUS ON GOALS & RESET OBJECTIVES

REFLECTION & GUIDED SELF-ASSESSMENT QUESTIONS

What are some of the big traumas in your life?

How can you re-evaluate these traumas, exploring the logic and emotions behind them?

What inspiration flows forth from these re-evaluations?

How can you flip into a "work" mindset when things go wrong?

What tools can you place in your arsenal to pull you out of the darkness?

Taking an honest look inside, what are some invisible wounds that you have left untreated as you increasingly step int the darkened void?

Who will you reach out to when you have lost sight of your paper trail in the void?

Identify some people in your local scene that might be living with invisible illnesses. Take the time to get to know them, and know them beyond their illnesses.

What random act of kindness can you extend to brighten the day of someone who could possibly having a difficult time?

SUSTAIN

EATING AN ELEPHANT
COPING WITH LARGE SCALE PROJECTS
& A SEA OF NEVER-ENDING TASKS

As I briefly mentioned in the Forward of this book, one of my father's favourite adages is "How do you eat an elephant? One bite at a time." I don't think people are actually eating real elephants in the modern day, but this old African proverb hold immense metaphorical value.

In the same day, week, month, year – I we are several different hats – audio engineer, manager, booking agent, performing artist, designer, dutiful daughter, writer, composer, friend, mentor, peer counsellor, collaborator, team member, citizen, consultant, and brand manager. My situation is in no way unique, modern humans are faced with taking on multiple roles in their daily lives and frequently become overwhelmed with the totality of what must be conquered in a short amount of time because our tech-centric society is largely evolving faster than our species.

The most important task at any given moment, is the one presently at hand, the bite you are consuming right now. How do you focus on one thing intently when there are a bevy of things that also require your attention? My father is one of the hardest workers that you will ever meet, and his detail orientated memory is like a steel trap. After a career in sports, my father worked at a Fortune 500 company where he quickly rose through the ranks to oversee a large team of salesmen throughout the Southeastern United States. My parents spent the first part of their marriage with my father traveling regularly between St. Petersburg and Miami by plane. He had multiple offices but could always tell you at any point what was going on in a specific sector. How did he do it? For one, my father has always been an avid note taker, but beyond diligent record keeping, he is a master at delegation. When he was with the major corporation he had several secretaries and sales representatives to whom he would delegate tasks that he knew each individual could excel at executing, which cleared his mind for long-term strategy and immediate problem-solving.

My father had an entire team of individuals to assist him in a day-to-day basis, but you have the same power today; dearest reader, it is in your pocket… your smartphone.

If I didn't have my phone, I would not be able to do all the things that I do in a single day. In 2007, I was just starting college at Florida Southern and I recognised the value that the iPhone would offer to my future career long before others bought into the smartphone life. Today, we think of smartphones for their entertainment value, and their ability to be working devices that streamline our professional workflow is trivialised. In a single day, I use my iPhone, Apple Watch, and AirPods to conduct business at a level of efficiency only matched by my father's former secretaries. My day starts with an agenda which outlines my scheduled meetings for the day an app reminds me to take my medicine and vitamins, another app reminds me meditate, I get on the road and my iPhone prevents nonessential notifications from coming in while I am driving, I answer calls in the car using my AirPods, I double tap either earpiece and I have access to driving directions as well as the ability to dictate text messages and make phone calls. I can dictate my emails while on the road, Google Maps keeps me up to date on the most efficient route as well as the accidents ahead of me, I can access documents for meetings, and even give presentations from my phone. I use cloud computing, which allows me to have access to crucial files at any point and any location in the world. I keep my general proposals, press materials, presentation documents, and performance files on multiple cloud services as well as physical hard drives. I hold business meetings on my phone via Skype, Facebook Messenger, or Google Hangouts. My travel arrangements are booked through airline and car rental apps on my phone. My airline tickets sync to my Apple Watch, I get scanned by TSA and the airline without ever unpacking my bag or missing a step. I pay for my morning coffee with my watch, and my physical wallet never leaves my bag, but most importantly, I don't waste time fumbling to find my wallet and then the card I want to use, or exposing myself to a thief who has physical access to my wallet. My watch reminds me when I need to wrap up one meeting and move to the next with subtle haptic pulses, it also gives me a brief window into whether a message that comes through on my phone during a meeting requires my immediate attention. At the same time, my phone assists me with winding down and getting a good night of sleep with scheduled downtime that prevents the usage of nonessential apps, and partners with my Do Not Disturb mode, which silences all nonemergency notifications until a specified time in the morning. Even the book that you are reading at this very moment, took advantage of the advanced features of my phone that allow me to edit, annotate, and sync changes to iCloud Drive.

When I consider all of the things that my devices do for me in a single day, I am grateful not only for the organisational features that afford me more minutes in the day as well as the safety features that keep me out of harms way. As a business person[9], the most important investment you can make to see improved productivity, is a quality smartphone and the time to learn the organisational features of that device. When you don't have to waste time wondering if you missed an important meeting or fumbling to find a physical journal, your mind clears for brainstorming and other possibilities; moreover, you are a much more present person when interacting with others because you only have to focus on the task at hand. Present people are inherently more invested in conversations, which projects a level of passion and investment in projects that clients find appealing.

As much as I am a large advocate for what my dad calls "maximum usage of available resources" where technology is concerned, I am still an avid proponent of pieces of paper. I love notebooks and use them extensively when it comes to brainstorming tour routes, keeping notes on contacts for potential contracted work, and meeting key points. I still write most of my acoustic works at physical instruments (primarily piano, toy piano, or Indian harmonium) and notate everything on custom manuscript paper that I designed in Adobe Illustrator years ago. I write letters to friends on Crane Stationary half page Ecru coloured paper at least once a fortnight, and send them out via First Class Mail. Technology opens up the possibility for us to explore the slower paced and artistic side of our lives, it does not erase these essential tenants of being human bur rather streamlines the mundane so that we can be extraordinary.

---

[9] While I use the term "business person" quite extensively in this chapter, the techniques and tools still apply to those who would consider themselves artists and homemakers.

Your electronic device can only react to the information that you feed it, so to maximise the usefulness of your organisational devices, we have to return to my father's time management strategies.

Always confirm your appointments via phone (or email) before heading out on the road.
Most of the strategies I've learned from my father are about the conservation of resources. This precept is primarily about saving time, because time on the road is ultimately a waste if your contact is not there for the meeting. I think as a whole my generation does not use the phone enough, by which I mean, we don't actually call people on the phone. As anxiety inducing as phone calls might be in the beginning, they are a crucial point of streamlined communications, what takes five emails back and forth, can often be solved in a single five to ten minute phone call. Why? Context, humans have evolved and been socialised to understand the meanings of subtle inflections of tone in speech that are impossible to communicate over email or text. YOU SHOULD DEFINITELY SEND A FOLLOW UP EMAIL, to confirm what was said in your phone conversation, so that everyone is on the same page, but a single *"as per our phone conversation on _____ we came to the agreement that _____ ..."* email takes less time and centralises key points far better than a thread of messages. Text messages should always be avoided if possible, when dealing with important matters because (next to Facebook Messenger) it is the least professional mode of communication AND it is very easy for important information to be lost in a string of messages with no seeming end. Most email accounts today will offer you the option to automatically sync events to your calendar if they are discussed in an email, which cuts down on the steps of copying and pasting information from your email into your computer. You can also, create email invitations for meetings, but phone calls show a level of initiative and investment in the matter that other modes of communication cannot convey.

Always start your day with the geographically farthest meeting, and work backwards to your office or home base.
Petrol is more expensive now than it was when my father was selling copiers back in the day, so this became a more pressing issue for me as I sought to grow my career; if you start with the farthest place and work backwards you will waste less gas than going back and forth from

location to location without a clear route. Additionally, your farthest location takes the most travel time and stacking that at the top of your day means you arrive at the top of your mental game, rather than rolling in at the end of your day exhausted and less prepared to negotiate or present your product.

Telecommute when possible.
Thanks to technology, one does not have to physically meet at an offsite location to conduct business. Stable video conferencing services, eliminate travel time variables, reduce the cost of maintenance for your vehicle, and cutdown on greenhouse emissions. If you are able to establish a stable Internet connection, you have all the benefits of reading body language and vocal inflection that emails and text messages lack.

Prepare marketing and proposal materials in advance.
In a world where cloud computing, is easily accessible to all members of society that can get onto the Internet, storing presentation and general proposal documents on Google Drive, iCloud Drive, Dropbox, or a similar service is a smart plan of action. Not only can the act as backup copies in the event you lose your computer or portable drive; you are always prepared to pitch to prospective new clients. Few people give out business cards, and so initial contact happens via email. If you have streamlined access to your promotional materials and a cursory proposal, your first email after meeting someone gets straight down to brass tax and demonstrates your initiative.

Look for trends in behaviour and possible roadblocks.
Humans are by and large, predictable creatures. You can tell the people that are going to be chronically late for your meetings and adjust your schedule to allow you to complete another task in the space where you are awaiting their arrival or you can head them off at the pass by meeting them at a location where you know they are guaranteed to be at a specific time. There are the people that are loquacious and affable, who will ultimately take more meeting time than others, you can handle this situation with a clearly written agenda at the start of a meeting, and planning your notification for your next meeting to go off a bit earlier so that you have adequate time to tie up the conversation without making the other individual feel as though you are rushing or dismissing them.

When planning your travel route, avoid scheduling meetings that place you on the road at the peak of traffic or plan to leave earlier if you can't avoid the traffic.

Just do it.

Sometimes we aren't at our best. Sometimes we are having a horrid day. Sometimes we are unhappy about circumstances. Sometimes we just don't want to do a certain task. In these moments, we have to pull ourselves up by our bootstraps and give ourselves some tough love. Things don't just fall off of our to do list because we ignore them, as much as our culture seeks to avoid confronting things head on, it is our ability to push through when the going gets tough that allows us to redefine ceilings and break new ground above. The key with this tenant is that you have to identify the things that you tend to shirk, so that your conscious mind can be present in the act of tough self-love that tells you to get the task done.

Know when and how to as for help with something above your pay grade.

Just because YouTube tells me how to fix my carburettor, does not mean that I should do it. Remember phone calls? This is another crucial place to pick up the phone. If something is broken or beyond your skill set, there is no shame in asking for assistance. However, you should always get multiple quotes and interview several candidates before you employ an expert to assist you with your problem. I drive an old Mercedes-Benz. I love the way it drives and the classic look of the car, but most of all, I love that I own it outright and that means I am empowered to work with my dad to make decisions on the maintenance of the vehicle. We have several car shops that we work with to maintain my steel chariot, and we don't just take the word of one because we've worked with one for several years. Sometimes we employ the phone book and several calls, ultimately ending up with a professional might not be in our regular wheelhouse of go to individuals. In the process of contacting competing companies, we are able to negotiate costs to get a better deal… to my father, a sticker price is just an initial negotiation point. While car maintenance and other purchasing decisions seem straightforward for this sort of lateral thinking, I carry it over into healthcare, and other portions of my life. I don't just choose one doctor or insurance or procedure based on the obvious course of action, I weigh my choices. There is an amazing feeling of empowerment when you make a decision based on what makes sense for you as an individual versus what is the expected norm. I like to think of it as going out to a restaurant... would you rather frequent the restaurant that only sells hot dogs and simply allows you to choose between ketchup and mustard; or would you rather go to the marketplace where you are able to choose from a variety of vendors of differing cuisines and a cornucopia of variations on the same cuisine?

EATING AN ELEPHANT
COPING WITH LARGE SCALE PROJECTS & A SEA OF NEVER-ENDING TASKS

REFLECTION & GUIDED SELF-ASSESSMENT QUESTIONS

How can you use technology to cut down on the mundane tasks in your life?

If you had a few extra minutes in your day, how might your self-care routine change?

Identify things on your list of todos that you commonly try to avoid or put off. Recognising the things that you struggle to push through will make it easier for your conscious mind and will to take over the motivation to get through these tasks.

RELEASE

EMBRACING CHANGE
LEARNING TO BE FLEXIBLE WHEN PLANS GO HELTER-SKELTER, GOING WITH THE FLOW OF LIFE, & EMBRACING MORPHING VISIONS

I love making lists, and I have a guilty pleasure of writing things down on index cards and then sticking them on the wall or spreading them out on the floor, so that I can clearly organise my ideas in a visual manner. My home studio has bins for specific cables and connectors. I organise my closet first by clothing type (ex. tank tops with standard strap sizes, or t-shirts) and then by colour, adhering closely to the colour spectrum. I suppose, I enjoy ordering my life in this way because I spend over half of my year in the state of perpetual chaos that is also known as touring.

Touring is difficult. Touring as a solo artist is isolating. Touring as a solo female artist is risky. Touring as a black solo female artist in the United States of America, is a dangerous undertaking that is not for the faint of heart. Sustaining a touring career as a single woman is probably one of the most empowering accomplishments that I have to my name, since DIY touring is an extreme test of survival in a modern world of comfort and convenience. Not only am I tasked on a 24/7 basis with physically protecting myself, but I am also responsible for the safety and maintenance of thousands of dollars of boutique musical electronic equipment from my personal inventory. Meanwhile living in the hyper-alert and hyper-aware state needed to keep yourself and your gear safe, a touring artist has to be amenable and "on their game" every second of their time on the road – you are on your best behaviour for organisers; you are maintaining strength for your fans; you are holding yourself to the highest standard of excellence for your personal artistic fulfilment while being aware that critics and cameras are lurking around the next corner; and if you are a black woman like me, you are aware that traversing certain areas of the United States is treacherous due to generations of racist rhetoric and a history of physical assault of blacks that continues into the present.

On the tail end of a long tour, I stopped at a Georgia rest stop to close my eyes momentarily, in the midst of a long night drive between venues. Actually, this was the second rest stop on the same stretch of highway, because the one that I had originally stopped at on the other side of the road to use the restroom in an emergency was basically abandoned and strange ghostly cats were skidding about the place… the creep-meter was off the charts, so I moved on down the road. Traditionally, I am pretty much against rest stops at night because they just feel like a Lifetime movie waiting to happen, and one of my dear uncles is a long-haul trucker so I tend to follow his routes and take rests at the truck stops that he has told me are well-lit and safe. Unfortunately, the United States is massive, full of stretches of road that are off the beaten path, and places that trucks don't travel. So here I am at the dimly lit rest stop on the other side of the interstate, that is at least populated with other vehicles including some trucks[10], and there were no spooky cats possibly trying to take my soul… so I casually turned off the engine, leaned the driver's seat back, and set a timer for a short rest. About thirty minutes into my nap, something told me to wake up… some would call it intuition, I call it a finely honed sense for weird nonsense. I normally try to tour certain regions based on the season, knowing that if I want to save money on a hotel by taking a nap in the car or camping out; the dead of winter or hell fire of midsummer, are not conducive for driving tours short on a healthy accommodations budget. Today, I'm really fortunate to have a lot of friends and hosts across the country willing to put me up, so the times I do camp out or nap in the car are quite rare.

This tour happened around November/December in the Southeastern United States and I was in Georgia, so the outside temperature was about fifty, but no more than sixty degrees Fahrenheit at the time of this story. It was about four in the morning and still pitch black, when my freshly opened eyes made contact with a lone man in a cutoff t-shirt and shorts akin to Rocky's training gear who began to do jump squats using the picnic table… I watched him momentarily, assessing the situation until, I started to see him run in an out of the darkness around the perimeter of the rest stop. Immediately, I turned on the car blared TLC as loud as possible without hitting the hearing damage threshold, backed out of the parking space and made a hard right back onto the interstate.

---

[10] Pro-tip pay attention to where the truckers are because they have more knowledge about the road ahead than you do.

Did I get the rest that I really needed to make it to my next planned stop? No... Did adrenaline probably get me to my next stop? Heck, yes! Could the guy just have been a random trucker doing exercise at four in the morning in the cold in Georgia in early winter? Maybe... Was it worth sticking around to find out? Absolutely not! Plans change in an instant, and you have to be flexible, assess the situation, and when you do act you must have confidence that comes from the power place of informed decision, rather than fear.

While I currently fly for concerts, at least once a month I find myself at my home airport, Tampa International Airport; I started my career with road tours. First off, I have done all the numbers for years enough to say that renting a car for long-haul tours is the most economical route, because you avoid additional wear-and-tear on your regular vehicle. If you break down, the rental car service will take care of the expenses to repair the car and generally switch you into a new vehicle. When you look at the cost comparison of touring on a rental versus using your own personal car, the savings are undeniable. Driving through most of the continental United States, and one cannot help but appreciate the vast wild lands, the organised beauty of agricultural crops, the unexpected wildlife, the mountains, the rivers, the lakes, the bayou... There is a meditative state that comes with watching all of these things whiz past your windows, the slow alteration of the landscape; a feeling that you are a small interconnected part of the morphing. I cherish these contemplative touring moments when I am truly alone, not answering phone calls, not responding to emails, just losing myself in the scenery and soundtrack of the road. Here are the moments that I fully check in with myself... Here are the moments when I feel extra blessed to be literally on my purpose path... Here are the moments that I am genuinely grateful for the incredible gift of life that we have been given...

At home, things are always in a state of change, I am constantly reminded of this fact when I return from the road to see new buildings, new businesses, and new ventures. In every community there are things that are stagnant and resistant to change, there are people that have become the darlings of gatekeepers, people that are unfairly afforded all the opportunities, because nepotism is real; and actually trying to engage disenfranchised populations is work that many people at the top of community food chains are unwilling to add to their list of things to do.

In January 2018, I had a short drive to return gear back to my home-base in Florida, that I had temporarily left with a friend in Georgia, while I continued on a flying section of tour for a couple of days. The drive from Athens, GA to Saint Petersburg, FL is an easy one, if you leave during the day and take the back roads through Macon thus avoiding the seventh circle of hell known as Atlanta traffic. As I neared home and the Sun began to dip below the horizon, I felt empowerment radiating through my bones and a high vibrational energy, like nothing I'd experienced before. When I had embarked on this tour at the beginning of the month, I was dealing with harassment from local artists who were all about complaints without action. Since I ended my association with these individuals they have either fallen into a void never to be heard from again or are still around regurgitating the same uninspired material for the same gatekeepers that I opposed when I left. I had gone out into the big bad world, after a year of being tied to my local community for lopsided collaborations that took more from me than they gave... after receiving harassing emails from disgruntled former collaborators... I left the Bay, took a turn in the ocean only to arrive back battle-hardened but otherwise unscathed. It was on this return trip, with the golden hour upon my rented Kia Soul, that I realised a change had come... and change was going to continue to come... and that I could finally release my desire to hold onto an arts community that was promoted as a diverse beacon of expression, but was actually a black hole of nepotism with cisgender middle-class white gatekeepers, who weren't actually interested in the concepts of equity, inclusion, and opportunity – but where this point, of rejection from my hometown by people that were not natives, and were not a part of the town when it had a struggling economy and unsafe streets; used to vex me and fill me with a sense of personal pain... as the golden light turned to shades of pink and finally red... I let go. I recalled the words that David Manson had told me about being an international artist. I recalled the freedom of being a single woman with no attachments. I realised that I didn't need to define my home by a presumed appearance of community. I realised that my vision of home and my vision of my involvement in home had profoundly changed... and that was an amazing thing.

Flexibility and the ability to change are also integral to relationships and mourning. When I started my nonprofit in 2013, I felt a great deal of push back from one of the student music organisations at a local university. In a good faith attempt to show them that a community organisation and a collegiate organisation with similar missions could coexist, I faithfully made the approximately 60 mile roundtrip journey from my house to the campus to regularly support their events. It was at one of their on-campus concerts that I met one of their leaders, his name was Sean, and he was bound to be a part of my life for longer than either of us realised.

It started with a simple Facebook message, congratulating him and his peers on a successful concert of new music; before long we were chatting over messenger several times a week for two years and Sean morphed in to one of my dearest friends. The new music world is globally a very small community and we are all fairly well acquainted with each other on some level the further you ascend up the ladder. My career had a bit of a head start on Sean's because I have been doing solo tours longer, and when he started planning his first few tours Sean looked to me for advice and recommendations. I made long drives from my home in Saint Petersburg to support Sean at his concerts in Tampa, and I made the personal sacrifice of going to a venue founded by one of my former abusers described in a previous chapter. I am an incredibly loyal person to the people that I bring into my circle of friends, the people with whom I express my most inner feelings, and as I had confided in Sean, early in our friendship – I am most comfortable with the written word. I would rather send letters and well-thought out correspondence as opposed to curt texts or meaningless ramblings over alcohol. Understanding that the written word was my preferred method of communication it is ironic that what broke us was not a shouting match but rather the written word. In 2017, Sean participated in the Orlando Fringe Festival, his first Fringe experience as a solo artist with his work LOCI, I remember him confiding in me at the Accidental Music Festival that was occurring during the same month in Orlando that he was woefully unhappy with his experience because attendance was low and the stress of breaking down his complex drum set and electronics rig was wearing thin on him. The month of the Orlando Fringe Festival and Accidental Music Festival that year just so happened to be his birthday month. Full disclosure, one of my favourite money saving habits is purchasing small gifts that can later be given to friends as well as family for holidays, birthdays, and other celebrations. I intimately understand the way it feels when you have invested time and money into a performance opportunity only to find the turnout to be less than expected... it for lack of a better term, sucks. Knowing what an investment Sean had made in Orlando Fringe that year, I started a secret campaign to make his last weekend's performances a hit. I contacted friends and former classmates that lived in the area, encouraging them to buy tickets to Sean's show. I told an elaborate white lie to Sean about not being able to attend his show, and then showed up with a surprise belated birthday gift as well as a note of encouragement. Dearest reader, I think we live in a time where displaying our vulnerable feelings and unwavering support of our friends with the written word is a dying art. I never expected that confirming how much our friendship meant to me would be the death of the closeness and frequent communication that bound us together from my vantage point. Less than a week after I penned the death nell of our friendship... less than a week after I went out on a limb to drive 2.5 hours to surprise a person who I called a dear friend... less than a week after I gathered friends together to help fill seats at his Fringe show... I woke up with the most intense chest pain of my life, it didn't subside – I was admitted to the hospital on the first Friday of June 2017.

I remember the events of what would turn into a three-day weekend stint in the hospital like a horrible movie that I wish I'd never rented from the video store. I remember the feeling of abandonment, and utter betrayal texting Sean from my hospital bed to little or no response. I remember trying to call him after I had a medically induced seizure on Saturday evening... I remember the feeling of avoidance, the cold darkness of isolation. Who will be there when you are at your darkest hour? In my case, it was strangers because the doctors concerned about a malpractice suit, told my parents that I'd had a slight dizzy spell but I remember the event completely... I remember my hearing disintegrate to a single sine tone... I remember my vision leaving... I remember my essence leaving my body... I remember regaining consciousness to a room full of medical staff, frantically attaching wires to my body and drawing blood... I remember the voicemail... I remember the sinking feeling when Sean did answer. I remember thinking that clearly we were not the friends that I thought we were.

Months later, I was practicing for an upcoming out of town piano performance, when unprompted I received a text message from Sean on the last night of his tour before he was due to return back to the area after about two-months on the road with his solo project. I could tell that he clearly had something to get off his chest, and he did it – in the text message where he told me that he wasn't in a position to be in a relationship with anyone. I was gobsmacked, because being with Sean in a romantic manner was not in my mind. It is something that has been posed to me by numerous new music colleagues across the US, because on paper Sean and I as a couple make sense – I get their logic – we are both hard workers, we are both independent, we are both loyal, we are dependable, we can read each other when others can't, we make a great team… and the list goes on. The only thing is that I spent years talking to Sean on a regular basis, we were great friends, but after a considerable amount of thought and inner reflection, I came to the concrete conclusion that as a romantic partners we could never function in a paradigm that didn't end in resentment; moreover, our mutual penchant for loyalty and physical intimacy would create a toxic cycle from which both of us would struggle to escape. Beyond running these hypothetical scenarios which relied upon a paradigm in which Sean actually found me attractive; I was keenly aware that Sean, like most men in the Western world, had no interest in a woman like me that lacked the idealised features of European beauty. So when I received a text thanking me for my vulnerability but stating that we should refrain from being in a romantic relationship, specifically that he wasn't in a place for a relationship with anyone at the time…I was flabbergasted and caught of guard. I tried through texts, to reassure him that I genuinely only saw him as a close friend. The problem with addressing these matters over texts, is that tone and context are lost. This conversation, no matter how challenging, should have been approached in person, like adults who respected the close friendship that I thought we shared.

We have seen each other multiple times since that fateful text exchange, and while there are moments where I feel complete in the ease and magnetic pull that used to be hallmarks of our friendship, there are many more moments where I feel a distance and tension that fills me with intense overwhelming morose emotion in the mourning for the depth that our friendship once had. I sat down to write this book in the fall of 2018, and I as much as I want to say that I am completely "healed" and have let go of that desire for a friendship that was once so central to my daily existence, I haven't. I don't fully understand why Sean and I are not where we were two or three years ago, and I frequently struggle with attempting to understand why he doesn't have a desire to work on repairing the bond that we once shared and I struggle to accept him on the level of a casual acquaintance or even less than that.

This story is one where expectations and miscommunications destroyed the fabric of something that was in my mind rooted in solid ground – his reluctance to confront me about what he perceived as a problem or issue, inevitably made me feel more distant from him; in turn, I accept culpability in knowing his nature and that Sean does not like to confront such difficult matters head on, in addition to knowing that he was going through somewhat of a transition in his life at the time, should have inspired me to be the person who took a firm stance from the beginning of awkwardness and sought a time and space for us to talk… I'm not in his head to know what he's thinking, but now we walk away from this friendship as two broken pieces of a common human sculpture once bonded by friendship, now divided by the words that we did not say. We often associate the bonds of romantic love as the most devastating to break, but Platonic love lost still carries a bereavement of unexpected fathoms.

When I first put this book into the ether, I took the time to sit with Sean and to address my sadness at the growing distance that he had placed between us. He walked away from that vulnerable meeting in a Florida coffee shop vowing to do more to communicate and to attempt to renew our friendship. He said he would text. He said he would make an effort. There were no calls. No check-ins. No hang outs. No effort on his part. We played a show together only two months after our meeting and then without so much as a phone call or a text message, he decide to move halfway across the country. Some people in life can't handle true emotion, true friendship, and true vulnerability – no matter how much you think you know someone or how certain you are of the bonds of a friendship – our perception of stable foundations, is just that a perception, that can shift as the sands of time reveal that the footing for our pillars was laid on unstable ground.

While my situation with Sean in the present is at times a difficult pill to swallow, it can be addressed on some level. There are on the other hand, forces that separate people from their loved ones with no recourse and no resolution. In commercial music school, I met a wonderful guy by the name of Andrew Roden. He was an incredible guitarist, a deep thinker, and one of the few people on this Earth that I felt I could confide in without judgement. For a time, we played in a jazz fusion group together, and took several classes together. I went to his shows, long after I had sworn off the bar scene. I wake up from vivid dreams of him wondering how things could have played out differently... particularly, I recall one occasion where something more than friendship was simmering... I went to a show of his indie pop band and we decided to continue the celebration at a nearby bar called The Bends. Nothing good in my life ever happens at The Bends, it is a weird vortex of just bad times. On this episode of *Reasons Why Elizabeth Should Never Go To The Bends*, I was confronted by Andrew's ex-girlfriend who told me, "I know all about you because Andrew is always talking about you." To this day, I wonder what the trajectory of my life would be like if I had been more comfortable being forward with men or confronted Andrew about what she said. You always think that there is more time to figure things out with relationships and people... my dear sweet friend was a Scientologist. Though Andrew never pushed his beliefs on me or anyone else, he was constantly taking jobs to earn more money for classes. One day, he disappeared off the face of the Earth, his phone number and email and Internet presence were effectively wiped clean. Scientology has a strict policy of disconnection from people outside of the cult once one signs a billion year contract to work for the church. I grapple with the lack of closure, the wondering where he is and worrying about his safety on a regular basis. Some days, I'm able to push through and just live, but the mourning of his absence is not like that of the dead – we accept death as an inevitability, as a part of nature, we generally know where we have laid our loved ones to rest. At the time of writing this book, all I know is that Andrew agreed to join the SeaOrg, that they might have assigned him to an office in LA, and that is it.[11]

Florida has the unfortunate nickname of *God's Waiting Room* because a large percentage of the population is made up of retirees living in planned communities throughout the state, including the infamous Villages on the I-4 corridor that has been known to make or break national and state elections for years, due to the sheer size of registered voters that are able to mobilise to easily accessible polling locations within the massive compound. As a Florida native, you spend a lot of your adolescence wishing to "get out" of a land that seems to be on the surface, devoid of meaningful cultural experiences. While many native Floridians, end up staying put or relocating to another portion of the state; a number of our best and brightest end up relocating to other states and countries altogether.

There are very few people that I can say have a complete understanding of who I am at my core, that know and value my heart. Even fewer people that I have an inexplicable very strong connection of understanding and unconditional loving relationship with immediately – call it friendship at first sight. One of the biggest internal adjustments, that I had in my adult life came when my friend Nathan Corder moved to California for school. I always say that Nathan and I met in the most Andy Warhol way, because we met at a venue at a storage unit in the middle of nowhere Tampa, that for sure wasn't listed on Google Maps. I credit fate and Eileen Sykes with introducing me to one of the people that would be so influential to my life, that I can't actually picture the artist or person that I would be if I had not met Nathan. Fate gets credit

---

[11]*I dreamt of you last night my sweet friend.*

I awoke to salty tears stinging my eyes and burning my skin.
The aching pain of a missing part of my world, lingering in my chest.

I can't pick up the phone and hear your voice.

Sometimes they've erased you so well,
I begin to wonder if you were ever real, or just a beautiful dream.

Sometimes, I wish I could stay a little longer in dreamland to feel your sweet embrace, to behold your enigmatic smile, to know where you are and that you are okay... but then my eyes flutter open and my heart sinks as you fade into mist.

because historically, despite my penchant and comfort for performance, I feel incredibly uncomfortable being in crowds, being around drunk people, and going out to events where I don't know at least one person attending. I remember that I happened upon the digital media show at Unit 17 because Facebook recommended the event after my friend Miguel had responded that he was attending – I never saw Miguel that night, and to this day, I have never asked him if he was ever there. In my mind taking a chance on walking into the unknown fulfilled a lot of my needs – I wanted to get as far away from Edison and the circle of friends that kept me in his sphere of toxic influence. Going to an event where I would be forced to meet new people that were out of my wheelhouse, and being in an environment without identity expectations, seemed like a logical solution to breaking the cycle of mental/emotional abuse that I was in at the time. I walked into the situation not knowing what was ahead of me. I also, drove into the general area of the venue without a concrete idea of where I was actually going. I saw some hipsters with some packs of PBR, took a deep breath to calm the anxiety within, and followed them, attempting to blend in with the rest of the attendees.

I checked out the digital media in the storage unit, and greeted the artists. Eileen asked me if I had come alone and clearly sensed that I felt out of place. She casually engaged me in conversation, and upon finding out that I was a musician, she declared, "There's another musician here! You need to meet my friend Nathan." It only took her a couple of moments to seek out Nathan in the crowd. The introduction was made. Eileen left us, and a strange settling of my anxiety instantly occurred. We talked about a number of things, we bonded over studying classical guitar, and a mutual interest in the works of experimental music artists, our choices of ideal graduate school programs, I can't be sure of how long we talked because time seemed to stop. No individual has made an impactful first impression on me that I felt a strong pull of energy and desire to see them again the way Nathan did that evening – not in a romantic way, in the manner that you just feel this person belongs in your life, in your tribe. At the time that Nathan and I met, he was averse to social media and didn't have a professional website quite yet. I actually connected with Nathan on Soundcloud, and to this day he's the only person that I have ever messaged on the platform. I invited Nathan to present his work for voices and snare drums on one of my community concerts, and then

Nathan began to invite me to USF new music concerts. Before long, I found out that we had mutual friends that I did not know about because Nathan had played in the band I and I with my dear friends Leo and Laith, but his entry into the group coincided with my withdrawal from the local music scene due to the presence of one of my abusers and the lack of support that I had received when coming forward about the abuse. When I start to trace my history next to Nathan's, the places where we could have met over the years, where we physically occupied the same spaces, or passed each other without looking back, are plentiful and almost eerie considering they account for almost twenty years of our lives. For whatever reason that Florida winter night, fate saw fit that we would finally meet.

Nathan started new music projects with my friends Danny, Leo, and Laith respectively, which meant that we were becoming regular fixtures around each other despite a literal bridge between our friendship – the three mile long Howard Frankland Bridge connecting my Saint Petersburg side to Nathan's Tampa side. Today, as a working artist, fully immersed in the international new music and experimental music scenes; I can tell you that there are a lot of talented people, but many are less than genuine or broken people lashing out at others. Nathan, has been one of the most steadfast fixtures in my life since he entered it. He has an authentic heart with honourable intentions. Our interactions have always been marked by a deeply profound mutual respect for each other on all levels of our shared human experience – intellectual, artistic, and personal. Never once have I worried that Nathan was lying or less straightforward with me about a situation or subject. When I was losing my mind about the first toy piano festival that I ever organised, I called Nathan, without prompting but hearing the stress in my voice, he drove to my house and stayed to help me entertain arriving artists and rehearse, even though he hadn't had coffee or slept. When I was admitted to the ER in June of 2017, I texted Nathan and he quickly responded with music[12] that he thought would soothe me during all the blood tests and battery of needles that I was facing – I hate needles.[13]

Nathan proved to me that there was type of friendship, where both parties had equal respect for each other, where both parties had mutual understanding, where both parties rooted for the other to succeed, where both parties looked for ways to incorporate the other in their success, where both parties were individuals and partners in the search for truth within each other and within the world. Nathan challenged my definition of an artist, he sparked my interest in Pure Data and coding, he introduced me to the music of Pamela Z, he made me feel safe while fostering a paradigm in which I felt the space to push myself to the next level.

It was because of the way that Nathan treated me – as an equal, as a human being with value and insight – that I felt the power to press on Edison, to demand that I was treated better, to hold Edison to his word, and that my expectations of a man keeping his word were not only reasonable, but a crucial clause in social contract of basic civility. When pitted against the raw honesty that my friendship with Nathan gave me; the inherent dishonesty of Edison's actions carried an air of cowardice that turned my interest in Edison into a distaste... by the time Edison yelled at me on that dimly lit corner in Ybor outside of New World Brewing, I wasn't looking for a conversation about pursing a relationship with him, I was looking for an apology for Edison's failure to respect my agency as a human being, and his careless manipulation of my feelings by choosing not to be straight with me about any feigned interest that he'd allegedly had in me.

When someone has such a profound impact on your life, it is difficult to imagine the world in which you don't have a regular interaction with them. I remember when Nathan told me over sushi at The Lemon Grass after a Sunday afternoon library concert featuring Sean, that he was

---

[12] *Good Morning Good Night* by Sachiko M/Toshimaru Nakamura/Otomo Yoshihide

[13] In order for them to put the IV in when I was first admitted to the emergency room, I had to put on *Erroneous manipulation* from Meshuggah's album *Contradiction Collapse*, on repeat. This has now become a tradition any time a doctor prescribes a shot, I have to listen to Meshuggah because if we are going to get brutal with poking and prodding – we might as well have a hardcore soundtrack to punctuate things.

going to go to Mills College in California. I can't exactly say that I was surprised. Nathan and I had talked about going to Mills almost since we first met, and I remember a distinct out of body movement at his senior composition recital at USF two years before the announcement over sushi, where I was hit in the stomach with a visceral feeling that Nathan was going to move to California. The news wasn't a surprise, but it rendered an immediate feeling of a ship lost at sea. I knew that Nathan needed to get out of the Tampa Bay area and go to Mills. I knew that this was the right choice for him. I knew that he really wanted to attend that particular school. I was so proud of him for the achievement. I was excited for the possibilities that were ahead of him. I knew that he needed to be in a place that challenged him intellectually and artistically. I knew that his departure would change the entire dynamic of the local experimental music scene. I knew that I was happy for him. Yet, I didn't know how I was going to exist in this new world where a person who really knew me, a person I trusted completely, a person I admired to the core – suddenly didn't exist.

I retreated to my primary coping mechanisms, I threw myself into my work, I went on tour, I rearranged my house, I gave a bunch of things to charity, I tried to avoid any moment of stagnation… I tried to distract myself from the hollow feeling that came with coming back to the Tampa Bay area, knowing that Nate wasn't going to be at a show with me. Before Nathan left, he'd penned a beautiful solo piano piece for me that I'd played with hesitation for awhile because of its subtle complexity of changing meters and the feeling of exposure that comes with performing spatial works – slowly, this piece evolved for me, it was a sonic letter, a sonic memory… when I played *Sashay*, it became a comfort a reminder of a dear friend… when I began to negotiate my first solo album on Aerocade Music, it was important to create an immersive experience that paid tribute to my journey as an artist and evolution as a strong woman. The inclusion of Nathan's piece at the beginning of the album, has a deeply personal context, that recognition the impact of a peer who saw my potential and strength, supported my eccentric ideas, taught me about different modes of artistic expression through observing his practice, and gave me the gift of a friendship rich in honesty – all the points that had helped me take command of my circumstances and define boundaries that created over a period of several years a safe space large enough to explore the sonic worlds that followed.

Today, I still miss physically seeing Nathan at least once a month for a local show, but I have become a strong advocate for his music. I have made a commitment to myself to visit him to workshop new works and just have friend time throughout the year. We talk on the phone or text, we find ways to stay in contact, and on the rare occasion when I feel the spiralling starting – I talk to Nate and immediately feel grounded amid a sea of laughs and serious conversations. And when we can't talk, I have his compositions to play, and the essence of everything that he would say in the space between the notes.

As predicted, Nathan's exit from the Tampa Bay area, caused profound changes in the scene. The effects that he had on everyone involved in the scene were evident when he left and people began to paddle around in circles with no distinct direction or trail to follow. The way I write about Nathan may make it seem as though he was a domineering and loud force of nature, but in actuality Nathan has a remarkable knack for guiding and inspiring others through subtle action and suggestion rather than brute strength. It is crucial that I point this out because he is a shinning example of a person who lives a resonant life, one that amplifies and extends to others, and one that fosters change in communities. While this book extrapolates on how I came to live a resonant life, it does not go without mentioning that there are other ways about fostering a resonant life and walking within your cosmic purpose. Even though Nathan and I approach the world with different personalities, different consciousnesses, different abilities, and different privileges; the common thread that we have beyond a deep respect for each other, is the firm belief that there is enough success in the world for everyone, and hoarding opportunity does nothing to advance our field, our community, or our core identities. When you stop looking at things from the perspective of what you can gain, and start looking at things from a place of the resources you offer another human that they might not have had access to without your intervention – you are living with purpose, you are living a truly resonant life.

During this time, I briefly had a duo with Leo Suarez, another pure hearted and true friend with immense talent. I met Leo through local shows with his rock band I and I right as I returned from living in Lakeland to attend Florida Southern College. Leo holds a special trophy in my mind for being the only living individual in the history of my compositional career that I composed a piece for, who didn't either become distant or turn into a total jerk after I revealed the work to him.[14] After Nathan left the area for greener Californian pastures, Leo and I started to work together on creating experimental duo pieces for toy piano and drums. Workflow and ensemble dynamics are always in a state of flux from one group to the other. In my traditional collegiate music studies, classical guitar ensemble and chorus class meant people working together reading from standard western notation. In commercial music school, I was one of very few individuals that could read pure sheet music, and in my jazz fusion group with Keirsten we often read from chord charts that I crafted. Leo's musical background was varied, but he wasn't a straight-ahead jazz player, nor was he an orchestral percussionist, and so we had to create our own working language for how to create new pieces that had some sort of consistency. This is when I started creating works that had specific cells following a linear pattern, that could be repeated at will and altered in the spur of the moment. Leo ended up creating a method of making notes on my scores and his personal lexicon grew alongside my own.

Leo also grew tired of the Tampa Bay area and ended up having a great career as a drummer based out of Philadelphia and traveling the globe, where he found the community and freedom that he could never quite grasp when he was in Florida.

Working with Leo today is another form of adaptation, since we have both grown immensely as players, the way we create has a new language but that natural energy flow is still there. In Florida we had rehearsals at least once a month, in Philadelphia we have rehearsal once every few months, and the aesthetic of the music we are writing together has shifted into a more mature realm where we have stripped down our rigs and focused on the preciousness of sounds. We look at tactics to take us out of our comfort zone, and we create rules for structured improvisations that require us to think outside of the box. Instead of creating a backdrop where I "compose" something that is

---

[14] *Leo's Song* released under my avant-garde electro-pop moniker, Suitcases of Sound, is also the first piece of music that I ever composed in Ableton Live with loops.

fixed and varied only by repetition – in the newest iteration of the Leo Suarez and Elizabeth A. Baker duo, we come to the sonic table as equal partners. In the first of our two Philadelphia rehearsals we were able to create the bones of an entire 45 minutes worth of music, to be fleshed out and recorded at a later date.

Making music across borders is not for the faint hearted, it requires a different sort of mental organisation. In your common musical group, performers may drive up to an hour for regular rehearsals at a centralised location. Your mindset for solo practice in between group rehearsals tends to be quite methodic, because you know what level everyone else is at in the immediate moment. When you are maintaining a duo or trio where performers have their own solo careers or other steady projects that keep them based in a specific location, your commute to rehearsal is often a plane flight or train trip, which is considerably longer than a simple hour drive each way. Most people lean towards an intensive week or weekend rehearsal with their ensemble members when maintaining a group across large distances. The way that one rehearses for a long distance ensemble is like running simulations in a lab, you have to practice the same material several different ways, and be prepared for your partner's playing style to have grown in the time between your last rehearsal. No matter how long you have been together as a unit, the first few minutes of rehearsal are like the awkward pleasantries that you go through when you see a close friend for the first time in years, and suddenly (never gradually) it is as if you had never parted your trademark banter repartee comes back in a single flood – except all of this is happening on a nonverbal energy level. It is a remarkable thing to witness, and even more profound when you experience the flip within yourself.

As a performer who's primary instrument is piano and toy piano, with my electronics and taking the back seat for a moment, I am always in a state of adaptation. You can't exactly take your own concert grand piano on tour with you, so I have in general played as many pianos as I have concerts... which is in the hundreds. Every piano has an individual distinct personality, some notes speak easier than others, some are incredibly sweet and bright sounding while others are dark and powerful beasts, some are muddy, some are crystalline, some are in between, some are tuned to A-440 others A-441[15] or in tune with themselves but certainly deviated from modern Western concert tuning. As a pianist, you are lucky if you get to have a few hours with the instrument the day before the concert, sometimes you only have an hour or so to become acquainted with this new instrument before the public arrives, the worst is when you have to walk on stage cold[16] and get to know an instrument in front of an audience. Drummers who perform on house kits, upright bass players, and harpists who fly for gigs and borrow instruments in the local area of their out of town concerts, also encounter this inherent need for constant adaptability. In the electronic realm, my work with analogue and modular synths offers the similar adaptation challenges to those that I face with new pianos. Analogue synths are finicky, like humans they need to warm up, and unlike their digital cousins, analogue synths can not store patches[17] to an onboard memory bank; instead the performer must memorise all of their patches, including where cables are routed and the exact placement of knobs as well as switches on the instrument – many of us document our patches in special notebooks with diagrams of the synths. Patchbooks, as these notebooks are often called, are incredibly helpful for initial setup and studio work; but you don't exactly have enough time to pull out your patch book in the middle of a show to confirm that everything is in the correct place to replicate your patch – mistakes are made, and many times those mistakes are just "happy accidents," as Bob Ross would say.

I remember being on tour for a week and a half with my MOOG Mother 32, convinced that it was broken because I had followed the patch

---

[15] A-441 is not necessarily common for piano tuning, but the concert grand piano at The Palladium Theatre where I rehearse in Saint Petersburg, is kept at A-441 because the principal violinist for The Florida Orchestra prefers it that way, and his piano trio is in residency at the theatre.

[16] One memorable instance of playing completely cold was a solo piano concert in Syracuse, NY at The Everson Museum of Art, where a children's program was using the theatre right up to the moment that I was to walk on stage to perform. I recall being personally unhappy with this performance because it was during the winter cold, and my joints were stiff for the first half of the concert. Although the audience and organiser were pleased with the concert, inwardly I was frustrated with myself.

[17] Patch is a term that we use in the electronic music world to denote the physical or digital routing that occurs to make a signature sound on a synth. The use of patch as a term comes from the days of large modular synthesisers built by Bob Moog and Don Buchla that had required physical cables to be plugged into patch bays on the instruments to create or alter sounds.

exactly as I'd memorised it. This tour passed through Asheville, and I was hoping to get into the MOOG Factory to get it fixed... in general, if you are an artist on tour and come through the factory with a malfunctioning instrument, they will try to get you up and running while you are in town. Just when I had rerouted my entire plans for the following day to visit the factor right as they opened, I realised that the LFO was set to the wrong waveform... nothing was wrong, except human error... but the piece had evolved into a profoundly different form because what should have been a continuous drone, had "breath" and "space" in between the bass utterances. For the week and a half that I was convinced that the MOOG was broken, I interacted with the ensemble and the curvature of the overall work in a different manner sonically... but I learned some profound things about how the work could rollout.

Circling back to situational flexibility, we can see that the immediate effects of our altered narrative and approaches to stressors yield an overall positive energy that makes us further prepared to take new hurdles – overtime this new outlook results in an emotional/mental endurance that makes the hurdles easier to get over.

During one of my first heavy driving tours, I was about an hour outside of Atlanta where I was slated to perform that evening when I got a call from the organisers, "How necessary is it for you to have a real piano for your performance tonight?" I answered that the piano was crucial to the performance because a lot of my work as a soloist involves extended techniques that require me to have access to the strings. The venue had purchased a piano before agreeing to program me, and was initially very excited to have me as a guest artist for their first official piano concert with this new instrument. People who are not familiar with piano maintenance don't consider that a piano is essentially a machine, and just like your car it requires regular upkeep, so I shouldn't have been surprised that they only pulled the plastic off of the instrument on the morning of the performance – unfortunately, when they "unwrapped" this second hand piano the pedal mechanism fell off the piano and they discovered other suspect damage to the instrument. While I was filled with trepidation as I drove past the Atlanta airport; I had already begun to run simulations of alternative ways to work my set just in case the venue was unable to secure a new piano before my concert that evening.

As I mentioned earlier, a pianist is one of the few musicians that is faced with the unusual task of learning the unique specificity of each instrument at every venue, and often tackle this undertaking with an extremely limited amount of time. In a case where a piano has just been purchased that day (which is what the venue had to do in order to make my concert possible) and then transported to a new climate, where in this circumstance it was partially exposed to the elements because the door jam near the large historical doors that sat at the back of the stage emptying into the Atlanta downtown streets had considerable dry rot. The odours of the urban night, discarded refuse and rancid urine, crept into through the large fissure as sulphur gasses from an active volcano waft onto adjacent neighbourhoods, and along with the pungent scents of the city, the cold encroached upon a space with the heater on full blast. Most acoustic instruments are averse to climate change and pianos, are notoriously temperamental with regard to humidity shifts, so all of these elements coalesced into a pressure cooker that resulted in the piano's keys changing response over the course of the concert along with the entire piano slowly going out of tune with itself… a veritable nightmare for any professional concert pianist, because we are particularly attuned to these subtleties.

Comfort is a luxury that is afforded to few gigs, more often than not, we end up being offered a storage closet as a "green room." I've made do with less than stellar accommodations before, but when I walked into this particular venue to set up, I was taken aback by how filthy the space was, and texted several photos of the space to my mum with the comment "I don't want to touch anything…" I recall that the rugs that I carry with me on driving tours smelled so disgusting after the concert at this venue that I drove straight through for six solid hours from my next show in Panama City to the late night convenience store near my house in Saint Petersburg to purchase a large container of Tide laundry detergent. My father awoke to see me at 4:00am with rugs spread across the driveway covered in suds, me using the hose on the highest setting, trying desperately to sanitise my rugs amid sleep deprivation. After my compulsive rug cleaning spree, I began wiping down and spraying all of my gear in what has become my traditional post-tour sanitisation ritual. While I am super flexible in most areas, I have to say that this particular Atlanta venue followed closely by one in Orlando are on my list of gross sketchy places to avoid booking or attending shows.

Adaptability and resilience are fundamental to my job, from the ability to get off of a long haul flight with a chorus of crying lap infants to play a near flawless concert from memory, to adjusting to a menagerie of different instruments, to navigating new places on my own with different languages and systems of measurement, to dealing with difficult individuals — I have to find a way to "make it work" and for the most part, I'm pretty successful, but it can be a struggle of will. I am fully cognisant that you, dear reader, are probably not whizzing around the world living the often unglamorous life of a touring artist, but I'm sure that you have to adapt in your everyday life as well — whether you are a mother or father balancing career with your family life, a corporate employee trying to push through the barriers of your company, or just an introversive person who finds it difficult to interact with lots of people even though you have something important to express to the world-at-large. How are you going to overcome all of these possible roadblocks? You are going to learn how to pinpoint your gut response, and take the Google Maps approach to avoiding the 65-minute slowdown ahead.

While I've shared a number of anecdotes in this chapter about how I've had to adapt to my situations, this was to prepare you for the real work at hand. You are ill-equipped to adapt to any situation or relationship, if you have not take the time to evaluate yourself enough to have a general understanding of how you are likely to react when certain circumstances are placed in front of you.

I use Google Maps a lot when I am touring on the road, and I recall with great vibrancy, a time when I got stuck in the Louisiana Bayou during rush hour on the way back from Beaumont, TX. Google Maps is constantly pinging your location to satellites and evaluating the data of countless other users to create an idea of how much traffic is on a given route at the present moment, and then analysing that data against the known thoroughfares in your area. While Google Maps initially tells me outrageous things such as "there is a 80 minute slowdown, you are still on the fastest route…" it will eventually update to say something along the lines of "we've found a faster route…" and lead me down the alternate path. The bridge that goes through Big Bayou is long and feels like the drive on the old bridges to Key West – rickety, unsafe, and forever. When Google Maps told me it had found a route that would cut 30 odd minutes off of my drive, I eagerly took it and prayed that as the Sun set on the marsh, I wasn't about to enter a parallel version of the movie *Deliverance*. To live our most efficient lives, we have to take detours past the 80 minute slowdowns within ourselves, but just like Google Maps, a detour isn't immediately apparent and we have to consistently scan and check against past knowledge to find a useful way to navigate our emotions and the responses of others.

I know that when I have worked for 20+ hours straight, I go into a mode where I'm hyper-focused in "executive mode" in which I become closed and obstinate to "frivolous emotions and meaningless tasks." I know that in such circumstances, I do not want to engage with other humans, and the best way for me to navigate my way is to put my headphones on or turn up the music in the car and focus on getting to a place where I can either meditate or go to sleep. Because I am aware of my behavioural tendencies, I am able to avoid snapping on people or being otherwise unpleasant; I put an extra effort in to smile and be pleasant to flight attendants or hosts. I also know that in this state the best way for me to navigate my present Maslow's hierarchy of needs is to focus on the present task and then transition to the next task without living in the emotions of the last moment, no matter how good or bad things might have been. Google Maps is not concerned with the data of the road already traveled other than to record that data for other users that are geographically behind you on the same route – once you have traversed a path, with a pressing deadline and destination ahead, there's no point in turning yourself around to recover the same ground.

We live in a society that hasn't quite gotten the hang of handling emotions, everything comes with a trigger warning while simultaneously shunning the embrace of individual emotion – we can be stirred as a unit, but individual declarations are not for public consumption and should be locked away from view – at least this is the general paradigm that we have created at present. Emotions are not wrong. Stress is not wrong. The only thing that is truly wrong is when we express our pent-up feelings in toxic ways that harm others. Once we have identified the triggers and causes of our unrest through careful observation, we are able to strategise methods for handling ourselves and fashioning a detour around negative outbursts that tend to harm us as much, if not more than we harm others.

EMBRACING CHANGE

LEARNING TO BE FLEXIBLE WHEN PLANS GO HELTER-SKELTER, GOING WITH THE FLOW OF LIFE, & EMBRACING MORPHING VISIONS

REFLECTION & GUIDED SELF-ASSESSMENT QUESTIONS

What are the most stressful things you encounter on a regular basis?

What is your typical negative response to stressful situations or irritating people?

How can you create a detour from your typical mindset or behavioural response to stressful situations navigate smoother roads?

Who are some toxic people that have tried to pull you off of your purpose path? How did it make you effect your ability to function with a level head?

What are some things that you could have changed about these past toxic interactions to create a new positive narrative going into potentially challenging future interactions?

Who are some positive people in your life or individuals not yet in your life, but that you think could have a strong positive impact? How can you reach out to them?

Understanding that everyone has a different capacity for friendship, create a list of standards for how you treat close friends, casual friends, and acquaintances; then consider what qualities you desire from the people on the other side of your platonic relationships.

_____
_____
_____
_____
_____
_____
_____
_____
_____
_____
_____
_____
_____
_____
_____
_____
_____
_____
_____
_____
_____
_____
_____
_____

Remember that Google Maps is largely made more efficient by increased data from users – be kind to yourself, your navigation around difficult matters isn't going to be perfect – give yourself some space to improve over time!

DOWNS & DOLDRUMS
UNDERSTANDING HOW TO NAVIGATE
THE LOWS & LULLS WITHOUT LOSING MOMENTUM

Most people have some experience with depression, whether or not it is chronic or clinical. Scientific studies acknowledge that musicians and artists face special circumstances that exacerbate mental health issues. You can find several scientific sources in the back that informed my decisions about how to proceed with managing my own mental health. For now, I want to deal with mental health on the personal level through the lens of my own experience. As I have intimated in earlier chapters, an artistic career has a paradigm unlike most jobs, especially when working independently in the field because you don't have sick leave, paid vacation time, a reliable income that makes planning for the future possible, reasonable assurance of job security, employer provided health insurance, retirement plans, substitutes for emergencies, and a whole host of things that conventional employment offers. While one can seek to fill in the gaps of a lot of these deficiencies, such as retirement planning and health insurance; artists still live in a paradigm where they are working ALL THE TIME.[18] On more occasions than I can count, I have been so intensely physically sick to the point of nearly passing out; and somehow pulled myself together enough to play by all standards a phenomenal concert experience for an expectant crowd. On the other side, I have had mentally trying states of depression or other personal disturbances, and pulled off a flawless interview with the press that made it seem as though my life was nothing less than perfect.

We don't like to see the cracks in our heroes. We don't like to acknowledge the humanity of the people that we place on pedestals. We place pressure on public figures to be perfect role models, and admonish them immediately when the fall from the grace of our idyllic

---

[18] People love to throw around the phrase, "Find something you love and you will never work a day in your life!" around like they are rappers in a club making it rain dollar bills. The truth is that when you follow your passion, every day and every moment is invested in work. You are constantly thinking about your next projects, how you can edit current projects, trying to figure out how to secure your next contract, how to market yourself, how to grow your business... there is no end to working when you pursue your passion. It doesn't mean that you don't love what you do, others just need to understand that when you work for yourself, the company hours are not 9:00am to 5:00pm Monday through Friday with holiday or vacation time — when you work for yourself, business hours occur essentially every moment that you are awake.

perceptions. Cultural and societal pressure related to my parent's station in life placed enormous emphasis to be "perfect" for my entire life. Children were to be seen and not heard. Acting out was never an option. Conversations in mixed company should exclude uncouth topics of sex, politics, or bodily functions of any type. Never discuss what goes on behind closed doors. Never show emotions in a large or grandiose manner. Speak and be cordial, but never loquacious. Due to the strict imposition of all of the aforementioned rules during my rearing, I notoriously keep my true feelings guarded through a well-honed habit of coat-switching. It isn't okay for me to be "not okay" because there are people constantly looking to me for strength and wisdom. In fact, a professor actually pulled me aside in college and told me that it was not okay for me to have a bad day even if I tried to hide my feelings by withdrawing into myself to avoid a scene. Our society tells women to smile, even when they are in pain, and we expect more of a toothy grin and sparkling eyes from those whom we look to as a light in dark times. The truth is that somedays, I need a personal day of reflection. Somedays, I don't have a Riley Freeman style quotation to wrap up this episode of *The Boondocks* that we call life. It took me until age 28, and a near death experience to begin giving myself the permission to be "not okay."

When you are an emerging artist, it can often seem as though there are more dark days than there are of sunshine. Why? Because so much of an artist's self-worth is tied to their work and the acceptance of their work by external sources – peers, mentors, patrons, general public, etc. Additionally, emerging artists tend to have larger gaps in between periods of activity and professional success. It is in these pockets of inactivity that feelings of inadequacy often fester and become infected with deep lingering depression. Musicians in conservatory settings are often pitted against each other because of out dated academic models, and fall into depressive states when they are publicly admonished for not being the best in their studio. Entrepreneurs and those with creative startups also face immense walls of depression as they build their ideas into reality.

I've always thought about the world on a level that was much deeper than I let on, and I have had a profound gift from an early age to touch people with my words, to know just what to say to stir people to be motivated about the possibilities within themselves and their lives. My father did a great deal of motivational speaking to youths when I was a child, and often threw me into the proverbial lion's den on many occasions. As he wrapped up a talk, he would turn and point to me, and I would have to come down and speak to children who were sometimes older, younger, or my same age – a terrifying prospect for a nine year old. My father's insistence in placing me on the spot from an early age prepared me for a career in some semblance of the public eye, because I was consistently forced to experiment with new ways to reach an audience. Today, people frequently tell me about how finding out about my existence has offered them a new outlook on the trajectory of their life and the possibilities within it. I am extremely humbled whenever a student, interviewer, or audience member comes up to tell me about the impact that I have had on their life indirectly by just practicing my art. I speculate that it is these highs that lead to feelings of inadequacy as a leader or community advocate when I by my standards I fail on projects that require a large scale group effort and support.

In the spring of 2013, I made the choice not to attend California Institute of the Arts, and with it, I made the deliberate choice to invest the money that I would have spent in continued academic studies into my professional career as an artist. In my mind, taking stock of the facts that I had already begun to perform around the country as a solo artist, was losing considerable amount of time in the classroom due to travel which negatively impacted my grades[19]; it made perfect sense to avoid taking out large loans for more education when I could use the same money that I was paying out of pocket for tuition to invest in the cost of doing business – flights, rental cars, gear, accommodations, food, etc. Because I came out of school with far less debt than my peers, I have been afforded the freedom of not being forced into an adjunct professorship or other teaching job that would severely limit the time I

---

[19] It is a shame that very few schools make space for working artists to study their craft, while maintaining a professional career. I was at the top of my classes artistically and academically, but on paper my grades were slipping because I was missing class time to further my career. Many former music students, seek my advice because their schools did not adequately prepare them with the real world experience necessary to sustain a career in the arts outside the outdated traditional models or professorship or placement with an orchestra.

have to devote to my artistic practice.[20] Simultaneously, I saw a hole in my home community, the lack of a place for new and well-curated experimental music. I remember going to a concert in San Francisco whilst visiting with my friend and former classmate Matt Mitchell, where there had been a four hour and thirty-three minute concert of works by John Cage culminating in a contemporary dance performance with Cage's music. I was so taken aback by the ability of the collection of children under the age of five, who were in attendance and actively engaged in the experience. The fact that children as well as older sects of the population could be captivated by such experimental works, made me feel that it was both possible and needed to create a space with the community accessibility in mind. My biggest undoing in life is my giving heart, and here we set in motion the events that would pull me into doldrums, from which I didn't think there would be an end or escape.

Coming off of the success of my solo composition concert at St. Petersburg College, I wanted to do more with new music, and in particular, I wanted to do more to expose the community-at-large to contemporary, challenging, and experimental music. I wanted the sounds that academics were largely keeping within their own spheres to be made easily accessible to the population-at-large. From my vantage point, I have always held that programming assumptions about what people won't like, inherently deprive those whom are most in need of escape from the ho-hum or drudgery of life, from the rich experiences of physical travel to new cultures and lands. If my mum hadn't exposed me to imported cheese, water crackers, scones with clotted cream, or fine tea as a child, I would probably harbour the same distaste for them as many American adults or teens that I encounter.

We often expect that the same people who supported us in one endeavour will be the same people to offer us the resources to make it

---

[20] Adjunct professors have a level of instability under the current American college system that means they are barely able to make ends meet. As stable as people think that adjunct professorship might be, the reality is that many adjuncts are homeless or living like undergraduate students. Adjuncts often live without guaranteed hours or healthcare, and push through injury to teach because they don't have paid sick time. As the salaries for collegiate administrators are on the rise, America's university departments are seeing cuts of tenured positions and degree programs altogether. All of these were facts that I considered when I chose not to purse the standardised path of conservatory training into professorship.

through our next similarly minded concept. The reality is that sometimes people are either exhausted from the magnanimity of the original task, or can't envision the possibilities of a future opportunity outside of the tried and true approaches. When I approached lower level administration about starting a concert series of focused on new music, I was deeply insulted when I was told that there was a concern about locating someone who was qualified to curate the series – a job that I could easily have undertaken due to my already budding performance career that had me traveling from coast-to-coast for solo concerts, and a host of burgeoning professional relationships with colleagues throughout the world in a sea of contemporary music styles. The suggestion was, that my original idea be taken and given to the new band director to control – another part that irritated me because I have never trusted that this individual was genuine or had my best interests at heart; this was an individual that I felt was looking to use this newly acquired position at the college to increase their own prestige and presence. Ultimately, the band director did not even take the time to meet with me or explore the viability of a new music concert series that was accessible to the general population.

After bottling up my frustrations for several weeks, I had an idea – on the road, I had previously performed in public libraries; additionally, public libraries have the added benefit of reaching the most diverse samples of a local population. Performances at public libraries are less intimidating than those in a formal concert hall, which makes for a more inviting atmosphere for people who did not have extensive experience going to the symphony or opera. I approached the head librarian of the St. Petersburg Main Branch Library[21], she met with me immediately in her office and allowed me to start booking dates well into the summer of 2014. Just like that I was off to the races, and I had found a way around the issue of institutional support from the college. Even though I was able to gather material resources such as venue and instruments, I struggled to solidify monetary and physical investments from patrons as well as performers in the community – until the day that we dissolved the nonprofit in March of 2018, I gave most of my independent income to keep the company financially stable, and even went so far as to take thousands of dollars from my life insurance policy.

---

[21] Following the reelection of democratic mayor Rick Kriseman, the library has since been rededicated as the President Barack Obama Main Community Library of St. Petersburg.

One of the biggest stressors in life for adults, is financial stability. The American dream of purchasing your own home, your own cars, and owning things outright is an ever-moving dream target for the people in my generation – millennials. My parents were able to put themselves through school with scholarships, while simultaneously working. By the time my mum was my age[22] she had purchased a flat in London and traveled the world regularly. When my grandmother had a stroke while on vacation in Florida, my mum had enough money to immediately fly in to take care of my grandmother and within two years she had amassed the money to immigrate to the United States, she walked off the plane and purchased her Mazda 626 in cash as well as a home for herself in cash, she immediately enrolled in real estate classes.[23] Meanwhile, I come from a generation where we are slowly lifting the shame of multigenerational living and carrying debt because almost every average college-educated millennial is dealing with looming student loans and underemployment. There are very few people that I know inside or outside of the arts, that were able to find stable employment in the field of their chosen major.

From July 2013, when I approached the library to March 2018, when The New Music Conflagration, Inc. shuttered, I lived in constant fear that I would not be able to pay my personal or corporate bills. I took a job as a substitute teacher that added to my chronic unhappiness, due to disrespect from teachers, underpayment from the school board, a lack of basic benefits for substitutes that had been promised to us in training, and secretaries that over-loaded work schedules by having subs work multiple teachers schedules at one time thus eliminating any breaks.[24] The final straw for me happened when I was covering for a band director friend of mine at a middle school, and was injured when a child forcefully pushed a metal chair into my shin. To add literal insult to injury, after driving myself to the urgent care facility in the school

---

[22] At the time I penned this book, I was only a few months past my 30th birthday.

[23] Although she already had a broker's license in the UK, she had to go through the same classes and tests stateside.

[24] This practice of eliminating breaks and cutting into lunch time, is completely illegal and violates state as well as federal worker laws; but substitute teachers don't have unions, so they have no one to represent them and thus, no legal recourse.

system's worker's compensation network. I looked at my phone only to find out that the school's secretary had docked my pay for the time that I followed district protocol and went to urgent care, immediately. Did, I mention that I was bleeding through my pants at the site of the wound? The secretary definitely didn't care about that when she docked my pay, and then expected me to substitute for the same group of children less than a week later.

On the surface, everyone was asking me to assist them with this or that project. On the surface, people thought that my annual toy piano festival was a success. People were not privy to the realities of festival participants that disrespected my mum, had little to no regard for opening my family home for participants to stay for free, investing in new pillows, bedding, air mattresses, food that was never eaten or barely touched – beyond the monetary sacrifices, I was overcome by the enormous weight of emotional sacrifice.

As, I mentioned earlier in this text, I had been told by people in positions of authority that I wasn't exactly likeable, and at this time when I was giving everything to build, to serve the community – I felt more isolated and alone than I ever had in my life. Moreover, it was tiring to keep a mask of contentment on all the time when I was hurting so much inside. All of these hidden feelings of career inadequacy were only magnified by personal criticism over my lack of a romantic relationship of which to speak. People who are pillars in the community, the ones that we place upon pedestals are not the ones that are supposed to show signs of a stress fracture. I'm sure that you can rattle off a sizeable or well-curated list of people that you hold in high regard, for the sake of those people to whom you look up; please remember that they are humans and have as much existential right to the roller coaster of highs and lows as any other individual.

For years, men were told not to show their emotions, to be strong and bottle up things that bothered them. Today, that looks like a father who I know loves me deeply, but isn't going to shower me with excessive praise or compliments. A father who doesn't treat me as his little princess, but rather busts my chops daily on the aspects of my career that could do with improvement. While there are many benefits to having a tough as nails Type-A father, there are drawbacks – sometimes internalising everything causes him to be bluntly critical of my actions and career choices – with a career that is already mounted in stress, has lead to breaking points where I go to my room and cry myself to sleep feeling lost in a fog of failure. My father doesn't mean harm, and he most certainly isn't abusive, but he doesn't express the softer side of humanity to me very often. My uncle and god-father is from about the same generation as my father. When my uncle had one of his first heart attacks my older cousin rode in the ambulance with him and tearfully confessed his love for his dad who was on death's doorstep. My uncle, though completely conscious and fully capable of complete sentences, merely replied "Yeah, yeah." In the case of my father and uncle, their definitions of masculinity shape the immense respect that they have for women, but they do not offer a healthy outlet for passionate self-expression.

While I have seen the positive aspects of traditional masculinity, in our present society we have seen how traditional masculinity, if not paired with feminist values, can lead to toxic masculinity, chronic microaggressions, and ultimately violence against women.

When people lash out against others, often it is a symptom of a deeper issue, and the lack of proper tools to effectively express the things that are preoccupying their head space

Profound and important messages don't come wrapped in perfect vessels. If you start to poke around history you can easily see that even the most seemingly ethical and groundbreaking individuals were either racked with internalised issues that lead to less than desirable public behaviour or private tantrums and breakdowns. Does the message immediately become diluted because the vessel is impure? In my personal opinion there are no gods on earth, and everyone has the right to fragility and fallibility – messages and thoughts, the basis of activism and movements are not absolute law.

In the United States, **affirmative action** was created by President John F. Kennedy through Executive Order 10925 on March 6, 1961. The order's original text states that race and national origin cannot be used for determination of employment. Thinking about the world in 1961 – the Brown vs. Board of Education Supreme Court ruling which lead to the official desegregation[25] of schools was only seven years old; President Eisenhower had sent federal troops to Little Rock, Arkansas to protect black students attending Little Rock High School just four years prior. The Civil Rights Act of 1965 that effectively made it legal for every American citizen the right to vote regardless of race, and outlawed discriminatory voting regulations that kept blacks away from the polls, was four years away.[26] There are 98 years between President Lincoln's Emancipation Proclamation and the decree of affirmative action. JFK was assassinated in 1963, just two years after he released Executive Order 10925, and because an executive order doesn't go through the same rigorous public debate that traditional legislative matters do, we are in many ways, left to fill in the pieces of what JFK meant this order to do.

For many people, affirmative action was seen as something of a "diversity quota" and I have vivid memories of public debates during my adolescence[27], where people said that affirmative action wasn't fair to white people who would have received spots at prestigious universities, if they didn't have to meet a diversity quota.

In the present day, we are constantly talking about "the diversity issue," and as I stated in a lengthy essay published by New Music Box in August 2018, and included in Appendix A – diversity initiatives are imperfect, they are marketed in a specific way that inherently ostracises others. Diversity is important; however, certain initiatives can lead one to questioning whether they received an opportunity because they were the best candidate or if it was because of a quota. A well-meant gesture by the leader of one of the most powerful nations in the world, has resulted in generations of existential questioning and a situation whereby the equity, inclusion, and opportunity that were meant to have been realised in our modern age through this historic law, are often tinted with doubt and displacement. Rather than being a melting pot,

---

[25] The Supreme Court ruling did not spur mass action to enforce desecration in America's schools.

[26] In the present day where we are constantly discussing women's rights, let us pause for a moment to recognise that the 19th Amendment to The Constitution of The United States of America was ratified in 1920 – a whole 45 years before a black woman was effectively granted the right to vote.

[27] By the time I was making my list of colleges to which I would apply, one is discussing a point which was almost forty-five years after the executive order was enacted.

we have "token" people that are somehow expected to equal out in a stew that has more parts of other ingredients than the paprika that you just tossed into the mix.

A great deal of my depression came because I was in many cases the token black person and the token woman in the room. In college, I struggled with trying to fit into the construct of a sub-society that was already heavily effected by stereotypes and leaning-tower power structures. Music school, as any graduate can tell you is not for the faint of heart – there's backstabbing and intrigue, crossed boundaries and competition; quite frankly, there's as much drama in the average music department as there is in an Italian opera. In college, I was another token diversity, one of instrumentation. I was the last classical guitar performance major that Florida Southern College had, and with it came a ton of undue pressure. Sometimes I wonder if I wasn't included solely because I was the primetime diversity draft choice. I was by my own admission a decent classical guitarist, others will argue for or against that position – in my own mind, if I had not been so heavily inundated with classes and expectations, I would have been more committed to the instrument, and perhaps these pages would exist in another format from another point of view.

My last year at Florida Southern College was a miserable one. I cried through the entire dress rehearsal for my final recital, and my teacher made me perform my works through tears. I cried every day that I woke up to the painted concrete cinderblocks and harsh fluorescent lighting as the fog of my consciousness lifted to reveal that I was still stuck in the reality of my dorm room in the middle-of-nowhere-Florida. I was fraught with feelings of inadequacy that tumbled into a deep depression. I felt as though I had no place in this world of music, and that perhaps I had deluded myself into thinking that I was talented at all. Coupled with doubts about my musical abilities was the harsh realisation that all of my romantic pursuits were in vain, that I did not have the build that men wanted and that I was at a loss to come across an artistic man with the wit and intellect to keep up with me – this depression became so intense there was a persistent pang in my chest, coupled with regular anxiety attacks throughout the day.

We don't talk about musicians and mental health enough, and my stick for that judgement comes from the fact that when I tried to confide in my peers about how I was feeling, they dismissed my emotions completely. One individual, whom I had trusted completely and regarded as a sister, told me that if I had any negative thoughts about something only bad things would happen to me – which, incase you are wondering, is the exact opposite of something you should say to someone battling depression and anxiety. Those words hung in the air for me, for years, and it was especially troublesome for me because my anxiety is not triggered by situational events. I have the sort of anxiety that seems to happen out of the blue, for no reason, I feel as though something very bad, and life-threatening is going to happen. In my humble opinion, doom-and-gloom anxiety is worse than situational anxiety because there are no visible or notable external triggers, just something in my body that chemically short circuits unexpectedly. So I lived in a constant loop where I would have a doom-and-gloom anxiety attack only to fall into a deep depression because I was thinking negative things, while I was constantly being told by a sister-like figure that the thoughts that I could not control were going to be my downfall.

At my lowest points, I felt that this couldn't be the only way, and that I couldn't be the only artist who has had difficulty in their lives. It was in my undergraduate years as anxiety and depression were building to a fever pitch, that I started heavily reading biographies of artists and the written works of John Cage and Arnold Schoenberg. I'd had a profound interest in Tibetan Buddhism as a child, but felt imposter syndrome around my studies because of Western appropriation of yoga and other Eastern belief systems. John Cage, was a cisgender white man and his embrace of other cultures was as pure as the driven snow. Schoenberg resounded with me because he is the father of pan-tonality in Western music. I found a strong parallel between social justice and music when I considered that in Schoenberg's compositional world all tones were equal, and defied the hierarchy of sound that has been so embedded in our consciousness that when most people interact with pan-tonal music as adults they call it atonal or noise or disregard its identity as musical sound completely. Similarly in Cage's writings he was completely abolishing the conceptual hierarchy of the West that ascribes to the belief that only the twelve equal tempered tones of the chromatic scale and the silences denoted by sixteenth Century notation, constitute "music."

None of these points are really radical in the world of contemporary music, but as a young artist, they spoke volumes to me – the idea that music was more than just what was contained in a theory textbook, resounded to the idea that a musical artist is someone who crafts with all the sounds that humans can perceive, and they are not bound to the confined traditional structure associated with conservatory thinking.

Biographies gave me an escape. Biographies were a subtle way of saying, "You don't have it that bad!" Reading biographies has an interesting effect on the imagination – I know that Beethoven is dead white man, removed from me by privilege as well as years, but when I comb through his story as told by a charismatic writer, I am for a brief time with him and identifying with his problems as my issues. The words provide glimmers of hope because he lived and he survived, are facts that come with an invitation with in the present mind that says perhaps the same can be true for the reader.

I figured out very early in my music school career that artists love to gossip, and that means keeping a good deal of information private as a means of self-preservation. The fundamental issue with holding things in is that when we don't have other people with whom we can relate or converse with on a meaningful level, small mental health and emotional problems spiral out of control into larger breakdowns and unstable behaviour.[28]

Having a British mum meant that, my life has always been attached to a concrete expectation of maintaining "a stiff upper lip" and the air of propriety that shuns the outward expression of emotion in public. In addition, being the only child of two parents who struggled to have me late in life, made me want to shield them from the darker trials that I experienced growing up and even into adulthood. The combination of these two underlying considerations, meant that I often avoided discussing the somber thoughts and feelings that I had at any given

---

[28] Studies in the UK suggest that creating a clear plan for touring artists of a chain of trusted confidants that are on call to let artists vent or discuss problems in a constructive manner can reduce large breakdowns, mental fatigue, and the likelihood of suicidal tendencies.

time. Additionally, there is a cultural consideration to take into account, because black families often dismiss therapy, and having an African American father from an older generation meant that his primary concerns were linked to tangible solvable problems, rather than those that lack apparent logic.

My parents, are some of the most loving and attentive individuals that a child could ever have been blessed with, because they thought nothing of sacrificing so that I could have the opportunities that they did not have. The first time I met Carol Davis Flynn, I was crumpled on the cold terrazzo floor of the school hallway in tears. I can't identify the exact comment or situation that lead me to sitting outside class, other than the fact that I was heavily bullied once I moved to the small Catholic school, and in an effort to change my impulse to defend my honour with physical tactics, I often found myself feeling warm tears of frustration welling up and my feet hurriedly carrying me as far away from the instigator of my saddened discontentment. When I wasn't running away from my class in tears, I was an intellectual holy terror… I finished my schoolwork quickly and was often bored thus leading me into mischief making during class time. In the 1990s it was all the rage to claim that all children had ADHD and that this was the source of classroom disturbances across the board, thus I was placed on Adderall like so many other children. My parents, fought placing me on drugs and tried several advanced methods including Biofeedback.[29]

I spent all of my middle school through high school years on Adderall until one day at age seventeen, I declared that I was tired of all of the side effects of the drug, poured the entire bottle of pills down the loo, and immediately felt a sense of empowered freedom paired with a hint of the doom-and-gloom anxiety that would become a hallmark of my future self. Being on Adderall was one of the worst experiences of my life, students who take it recreationally in college to pass exams and study harder have no clue of the horrors that the drug can impose. I had heart palpitations on a regular basis, my vision would telescope and focus on finite points of things like the baseboard in my bathroom, and at one point I was sitting in religion class during my senior year of high

---

[29] Biofeedback is a therapy process that involves attaching electronic monitoring equipment to the head and in theory, allows the patient to train certain functions of the mind. It has been claimed to assist some people that have issues with both mental health as well as physical disorders.

school and saw a three dimensional fuchsia box floating in mid-air as the teacher was giving a lecture.

On the flip side, Biofeedback was a sci-fi horror come true, and my only consolation was that my parents often brought my beloved akita Keeper when they picked me up from Biofeedback sessions. I realise that very few readers will have experience with Biofeedback, so let me briefly explain what I remember of the sessions that I had as a middle schooler. Every session began with a technician attaching wires to my head and then they would turn the lights off and a screen would have something akin to a video game on it. To this day, I have serious questions about how it actually worked, but it seemed as if my mind was controlling the game. The technician would monitor me from another room and afterwards they would print out a bunch of paperwork showing my brain activity and how it had changed across my various sessions. I absolutely hated Biofeedback, and in fact, I often found myself dealing with a ton of anxiety because their were no clocks in the room; I was always waiting on pins and needles to see when I could leave.

All of these early experiences left me severely disillusioned with psychiatry and Western medical practices because it seemed to me that all the doctor would do is prescribe me medicine after medicine. When I cried in the psychiatrist's office confessing to having chronic night terrors along with anxiety that caused me to wake up screaming, he simply placed me on another drug, BuSpar. Later in life when I started to do serious research into the side effects of the drugs that I was placed on as a child, it became abundantly clear to me that some of these chemical reactions stirred up many latent mental health problems.

The fact of the matter is that mental health issues are a real part of our society, and they aren't going away. In reading biographies of artists that toured extensively, I started to notice troubling patterns of lows and highs that were inline with a lot of my own personal experiences. I realised a common thread between many tragic stories, and particularly the tale of Nina Simone, is that in an attempt to keep pushing forward and present an air of strength, the red flags of serious mental health issues were overlooked to the point that when one sought treatment, it was often too late because the individual was so trapped by the paradigm of their circumstances that they didn't see a way out or feel worthy of escaping their situations. From a chemical perspective, I deduced quite early on that lack of sleep and other stress related environmental factors could lead to the onset of mental health issues that might have otherwise laid relatively dormant.

While I found a great benefit from homeopathic remedies including traditional Chinese herbal medicine, acupuncture, meditation, and yoga; I still grappled with vivid night terrors, but even further there was an ever growing persistent sadness coupled with feelings of inadequacy as I failed to have any success in romantic relationships – in fact even through age thirty, I had no romantic relationships of which to speak, a fact that made someone as goal and perfection oriented as I am, feel less than adequate. Acupuncture and herbal medicine quelled my anxiety considerably and in tandem with Western medicine, it seemed on the surface that I was a high-functioning success. Inwardly, I was unraveling… I have always been fascinated with trying to figure out why people make the choices that they do, and why they express themselves in a particular manner, whether good or bad in nature. The only problem with this fascination is that it triggers obsessive compulsive loops of analysing and over-analysing subjects or incidents that have been long forgotten by others.

For days, leading up to June 1, 2017, I had been hiding an intense overwhelming and persistent chest pain. When I awoke that Friday, June 2, 2017, the pain was so severe, I spent the first few hours of my day in bed in tears. I called my primary care doctor, only to find out that she wasn't around, but the nurses demanded that I come in to be seen that day. I was forced by the attending physician at the large practice I went to at the time to go to the hospital. I walked myself into the hospital, not realising that upon discharge, I would have a profoundly different life than the one with which I entered through the automatic glass doors of the emergency room.

It was in the hospital that I had a vasovagal response, my blood pressure plummeted and I seized. Less than five days before, I had been in Orlando to support my friend Sean in his first Orlando Fringe Festival experience. Though he greeted me in his own sort of cordial Sean manner, I felt his distance, and was inwardly despondent. I felt as though my care for others was worthless and by extension I was unwanted by the world.

For years, my primary care doctors had been prescribing me the anti-anxiety medication Xanax to help me combat the stress-based anxiety that caused my blood pressure to constantly be at a level that was so high it was almost untreatable. The problem is that nobody was providing me with a safe space to be open about my true feelings or experiences, and so I lived in a private world of negative thoughts that drove me to constantly push myself to be perfect while simultaneously beating myself up for every time that I fell short of perfection. It was at age 28, when someone finally listened to me after nearly dying… that they diagnosed me with high-functioning depression, and when I was finally placed on an antidepressant.

Medicine is a cooperative practice, it requires work on both the side of the physician as well as the patient. Many doctors have a bit of "God syndrome" they believe that they have all the answers and that a bunch of statistics in books and a sea of expensive education make them the masters of fate. The truth is that every person, has a different story and is a unique set of chemical reactions walking around. When I was first admitted to the hospital, I was assigned to a doctor who came in the room with an air of pompous arrogance that immediately made me feel uncomfortable. He began to demand a course of treatment that I knew would have side effects that I did not want to entertain. Little did they know that one of my oldest and dearest friends Luegenia is a professional licensed pharmacist who did her residency in a hospital, and another friend and former classmate, the wonderful violist who appears on many of my early albums, Dawn, is a professional licensed music therapist who works in a hospital psychiatric ward. I was keeping both Luegenia and Dawn updated on everything that was going on via text message. I was also channeling the wisdom of my former teacher and sponsor for Catholic confirmation, Carol Davis Flynn, who had taught me early in life that you don't have to, and should never rely on the single opinion of one doctor.

On the evening of my first night in the hospital, one of the nurses came in to tell me that the attending physician wanted to speak with me on the phone. With palpable condescension in his tone as he told me that if I didn't do what he wanted, he would place me in the ICU where I couldn't make decisions for myself — that's when something he never expected to happen occurred... I got mad. In typical fashion, if you irritate me enough, I'm not going to yell or make a scene, but the Brit in me comes out in full force to give you a dressing down. In a calm voice that carried the weight of centuries of noble ancestors, I said, "Medicine is a collaborative effort between patient and physician. You have neglected to consider my voice in a conversation that has become a monologue. Quite frankly, your bedside manner has been lacking and this conversation will mark the end of our working relationship. I want a new doctor." I then hung up the phone and with a cold air of detached propriety, I said to the nurse, "I don't ever want to see that man in my room again." At this point, the doctor was ashamed and he asked the nurses to allow him to speak to my parents. I refused that request, stating that not only was I an adult fully capable of making my own decisions, but that I had no problem calling my insurance company to life flight me to a better hospital. All of a sudden, the way the doctors at the hospital treated me began to change profoundly, they no longer spoke to me as if I was a child. Fear and respect was further supplanted when Luegenia came to visit. I remember she had made the sacrifice of carving out time from a family funeral to come see me in the hospital, and to this day, I am beyond grateful that she made me and my health a priority. When she came in the room, she started asking the nurses questions about my care as well as inquiring about the medicines that they had me on... including the absurdity of having me on a saline drip while trying to lower my blood pressure. Shortly after visiting hours were over and they made Luegenia leave they gave me a pill, and I began to feel... off.

I was sitting in my room, when suddenly I felt hot followed by nausea and a shortness of breath. I pulled the emergency cord and immediately a nurse who shared my same first name came to my side. She held me up and rubbed my back assuring me she would not leave me no matter what... she called for another nurse who put a blood pressure cuff on me and all I saw were numbers plummeting and my pulse barely registering on the machine. In this moment, my senses started to leave me — first, my hearing was replaced with the sound of a single sine tone which faded away into nothing, my vision began to grow blurry and tunnel until I was in a sea of blackness. My perception of time had long escaped me things were slow and then fast and then slow simultaneously. Briefly, I came to in a wheelchair, a fog surrounded my perception and I was confused about where I was... then just as quickly as I came to the world of the living, the darkness overtook me. Suddenly, I was in the hospital bed surrounded by no less than nine medical professionals, taking blood, taking my vitals, attaching wires to check my heart, they were asking me dumb questions that I knew because this second time I came back, I was fully aware of what had happened.

My spirit animal is a lioness, but sometimes I also think I have a bit of a Phoenix in me because the way that I bounce back from hardship has always been incredible to me. They asked me if I could see, I quipped that they had taken my glasses, so sure I could see but everyone in the room was blurry. In a moment of levity from the universe, the head resident turned to the crowd of medical professionals and asked if anyone had a pen light... in a group of over nine attending health professionals, nobody had a pen light... which is of course, is exactly the level of preparedness that you want to hear about when you have just had a seizure... so they had the bright idea to shine an iPhone flashlight in my face. After all the hustle and bustle, they turned the light out... my body started to go into shock... I was cold, even though I was covered with blankets and bundled to prevent further injury because I had acquired several cuts and such from my episode.

The hospital lied to my parents and told them I had had a minor dizzy spell, and it wasn't until I was at home later that week deprived of sleep because I kept waking up screaming every time my dreams faded into blackness that I finally broke down in a rant and revealed to my mother everything that had really happened.

I saw a profound sadness in my parents eyes, and at one point the day that they discharged me, I had another minor vasovagal episode while my mum was out of the house. My father, a huge strong man still with the build of an offensive tackle from his professional football days, had a look in his eyes of complete helplessness and panic as he watched me crumpled on the floor, not knowing how he could help me.

Looking back, the pain that I felt, and the pain that my parents felt, could have been easily avoided if my doctors had given me the safe space to express myself. When I got out of the hospital I became even more determined to seek professionals who would be willing to listen to me, and who would respect my wishes to try adjunctive treatments over a sea of synthetic substances.

After extensive research over the next year and half, I ended up with a care team that I truly feel is right for my health. I have doctors who listen to me, who make me feel as though they care about the totality of me as an individual rather than a series of textbook symptoms that they aim to quash. In particular, I have a psychiatrist who recognises that as a highly intelligent being, I analyse my own issues constantly and try to consider all sides of a matter, he realises that a lot of my troubles come from not speaking up and owning who I am for fear of retribution or further isolation.

For me, my antidepressant has given me a new lease on life, that baseline sadness and heaviness in my chest is no longer a persistent tormentor. What most people were registering as generalised anxiety has evolved into a full embrace of the range of human emotions from positive to negative and every shade in between.

I realise how incredibly lucky I am to be alive, because on the night that I coded the medical staff could not revive me because I have a very clear living will, which specifies that I do not want to be resuscitated. I firmly believe that if it is my time to go, then I want to slip into death peacefully and naturally. I also, never want to create a situation where my loved ones are tasked with the enormous burden of deciding whether to let me live or die. When they admitted me into the hospital at age 28, they staff were all taken aback that I had an actual living will that my mum could present to them upon request. I was completely cognisant as my senses left me, that I had a DNR (do not resuscitate) clause in place, and that if the universe saw fit that it was my time, my life would have ended on June 2, 2017. Processing such a traumatic event, is not easy, but I became resolute that my purpose on this Earth was not finished and that every breathe after the darkness was a gift not to be taken for granted.

Today, I recognise that there are a number of things that can cause us to feel down, and we have the tools to combat them. Some of us have inherent chemical imbalances that require us to seek help from licensed psychiatrists and take medicines such as antidepressants. There is no shame at all in seeking assistance from professionals or needing to take prescribed medication under the supervision of a licensed physician. The less we stigmatise mental health issues, the more we can move forward as a society and less of us will be faced with breakdowns that require critical care, under which we could possibly lose our lives. Through this traumatic event, I also realised how important it is to discuss problems and work through them. I don't always have to agree with others, but we can make a concerted effort to respect our unique viewpoints and approaches to the world.

The most important thing I concluded from this experience, is that depression, disagreements, negative thoughts, and other feelings are completely valid; people are not supposed to be perfect, we are all a work in progress. Instead of trying to dispose of people facing difficulties like we dispose of our cellphones once they slow down, we have to open our devices – open ourselves up and investigate the underlying problem. Sometimes to complete a repair properly we may need the intervention of a professional. Sometimes we can troubleshoot and solve the problem with help from a friend or two. Sometimes we have the power to work through the issues on our own. The primary takeaway is that we have to put in the work, and we have to create spaces for dialogue and we have to be prepared to try different methods. We have to rewire ourselves to become fixers rather than consumers.

DOWNS & DOLDRUMS
UNDERSTANDING HOW TO NAVIGATE THE LOWS & LULLS WITHOUT LOSING MOMENTUM

REFLECTION & GUIDED SELF-ASSESSMENT QUESTIONS

How often do you feel depressed?

_____
_____
_____

What triggers depressive thoughts for you?

_____
_____
_____
_____
_____
_____
_____
_____
_____
_____
_____
_____
_____

Have you reached out to others about how you feel?

_____
_____
_____

If you could talk to a professional councillor or therapist or impartial third-party, what would you say to them about your inner dialogue during times when you are particularly down?

_____
_____
_____
_____
_____
_____
_____
_____
_____
_____
_____
_____
_____
_____
_____
_____
_____
_____
_____

How do you normally cope with depression and depressive thoughts?

Would you consider your coping mechanisms to be healthy? Why or why not?

What are alternative methods for pulling yourself out of the doldrums could you try in the event that your regular coping mechanisms become stale and plateau?

Are there any stories of real people with similar lives that can serve as reminders that you are not alone, as well as temporary respite and escape from the troubles that you are feeling at present?

Take a moment to create a crisis action plan, this includes an easily accessible list of people to call in the event of a mental health emergency, a safe place or several to go, as well as supplies that one might need for comfort and medically. Make sure to write this crisis plan out somewhere and share it with at least three trusted people.

WALLS & COAT SWITCHING
NETWORKING & SOCIALISING SURVIVAL TACTICS

Growing up with a British mum, meant that propriety and social graces were everything. I often laugh when people think that they have made a good impression on my mum, but I secretly know that she has not been pleased with their lack of decorum. The Brits have the poker face down, and rarely show their hand to anyone. In my family, I was expected to know how to attend and host a formal dinner party by the time I was nine years old; at seven, I could tell you the differences between the continental place setting, a casual American place setting, white wine glasses, chargers, red wine glasses, champagne flutes, the flow of a meal, and most importantly, I knew the proper subjects for mixed conversation and never to insult the good name of my family by indulging in lewd topics or gaudy displays of wealth. Since my mum was the primary parent involved in my academic rearing, my diction and spoken command of the English language favoured as mother would say, "The Queen's English" – which largely equated to sounding like a proper British child within my home.

When I went to public school, my mum's European flair was not accepted by my classmates. I was constantly made fun of for the way that I spoke and because instead of bringing Lunchables to school, my mum often packed Perrier water, grapes, dry salami, brie, and either water crackers or a piece of baguette – which looking back today, is basically the same thing as a Lunchables kit, just without all of the processed chemicals and weird yellow things purporting to be cheese. After getting into a few rows on the playground in elementary school with other children who sought to make me feel as though I was worthless because of my cultural differences, I decided that I would alter my speech pattern, and diction in an attempt to assimilate within the American culture of school.

Ironically, I have always held steadfast to my proclivity to write in "The Queen's English" which, caused me a fair amount of trouble with teachers and administrators, who frequently thought that I was cheating because of my advanced sentence structure and lexicon. Even though tests had shown that I was an advanced learner, and later I was placed in the school systems' Gifted Program; I went through a series of trials where teachers and administrators who thought I was cheating, subjected me to writing essays on notebook paper under their supervision and time restraints to prove that the way I composed my thoughts on paper was natural. As an adult, I critically question whether or not there was a tinge of underlying racism and sexism in this process, because white cisgender boys who wrote at levels higher than their grade levels, were consistently praised; meanwhile, I just faced more tests and disbelief.

My American school experience was the first time that I knowingly engaged in some form of coat switching. For those not familiar with the term, **coat switching**, occurs when we alter our natural tendencies to survive within a group or social structure. We engage in coat switching practically every day, for general survival in society. You don't speak to your bosses, or potential clients the same way that you speak to old friends, family, or others with intimate knowledge of your private affairs. Just as we discussed with pack mentality in an earlier chapter, on the surface coat switching has positives, but in a society that becomes overzealous about homogenising the general population, coat switching can go horribly awry.

In my experience, coat switching has never had the same sticky dirty feeling that comes with masks, because there is an element of our true identities still embedded within the paradigm of coat switching. I was raised by a mother of European heritage, this means that I can easily mix in certain circles that are an assimilation struggle for my American born cousins and friends who haven't had the privilege of international travel. When I cross out of the United States, I down play my "loud American" traits, while I'm still a bit eccentric, I naturally adjust to a more conservative coat that fits in with the applicable European society.

Growing up in the pre-recession American middle-class financial comfort of the 1990s, meant that when my mum strongly disagreed with both the public school education standards as well as the administrators; she was able to pull me out of 5th grade at Bay Vista Fundamental Elementary School on a Wednesday, and enrol me in the smaller private Roman catholic school, Most Holy Name of Jesus by Friday of the same week.

Moving to a new school in the midst of the academic year is trying for most children, and it is even harder when one considers that my entire life has been an attempt at balancing the heavy European influence of my mum, and Latina influence of her mother who hailed from Venezuela; with the American ideals and societal norms that I encounter the moment that I step foot outside of my house. My father has a large family, and while extremely mixed as my mum's heritage, it is from my father that I have my African-American identity.

Under race on my mum's immigration paperwork, it says other, and my birth papers granted me the same ambiguous designation. I am an amalgamation of so many different cultures that it took me well into my adulthood to comfortably identify with my African-American heritage in a meaningful way. My mum had made a point to teach me about the history of Britain from a very early age, and while I was fully aware of the struggles that blacks faced in America, I was largely sheltered from these realities, because in private schools there are very few black children, particularly in what most diocese call "feeder schools" – the collection of neighbourhood K-12 schools through out the diocese that lead to a regional high schools under control of the Catholic church. It wasn't until I went to St. Petersburg Catholic High School, that I met another black girl from a similar middle-class background, who I'm incredibly blessed to still call one of my dearest friends to this very day, Luegenia Sherriffe.

People often assume that just because people share the same colour of skin, religious beliefs, or tastes in musical scene that these homogenised traits would lead to complete authenticity, and that coat switching would not occur. Let's break things down for a moment –

- I grew up in a middle-class household in the last height of economic stability the United States has seen in present memory.
- I went to prestigious private schools where minority enrolment accounted for less than 1% of the student population.
- My parents had me late in their lives, which meant that they had already extensively traveled and experienced other cultures.

- My mother is from another country with an entirely different set of societal expectations and mores.

- My only interaction with black children in "the hood," occurred when I was doing motivational speaking with my father and mother.

- Due to my mum's upbringing she reared me with a great deal of exposure to adult debates about politics, history, and avant-garde art. I spent a lot of hours in the family room listening to recordings of Stravinsky's *Rite of Spring*, and Prokofiev Symphonies.

- I was an avid reader, with a love for Russian literature and books on philosophy. I began reading Descartes *Discourse on Method & Other Metaphysical Writings* when I was in 8th grade, and by senior year I was combing over Kant, Henry G. Frankfurt, and the biographies of major composers. I never even read a single book from the Harry Potter Series or even The Babysitter's Club.

When one considers the realities of the world in which I was raised, it should not be a surprise that I constantly felt out of place with the other black children in private school, except for Luegenia. Sure I was a fan of Destiny's Child and TLC, but I had made a conscious choice to stop listening to the radio when I was in 6th grade because I noticed how the same few songs would always play on heavy rotation and deduced that there were corporations controlling our tastes. I decided, in 6th grade, that while I couldn't have agency over many things in my life, I could control the music that I allowed to influence me, as such I spent most of my remaining adolescence with a portable CD player and to this day, I still abstain from consuming the media on local radio stations. The one exception to my commercial radio abstinence could be my friend Steven Head's show on WPRK, but since it is a public radio station and I know that Steve's tastes are as discerning as my own, I've never really counted it as a relapse in my radio sobriety.

What do you do when you are a black child in a very white-washed world, while simultaneously feeling as though you don't fit into the same group of people that the melanin content of your skin and societal prejudice says you should be relegated to remaining in? You try to own your developing identity through adolescence, but it is difficult. I tried to wear the coat of a typical white American teenager, but I suffered inwardly with depression because my hair was too kinky, but most of all – I always hated my face and my body. I was diagnosed with PCOS[30] while still in high school and one of the primary side-effects that I experienced was the appearance of hair, that still grows under my chin today. When you are nearing 5' 10" with an extremely athletic build, the last thing you want to have to deal with is hair underneath your chin.[31] In addition, I really wanted to have the long beautiful neck that so many of the white women had. My body image issues got to a point where I broke down crying and begging my mum to let me have liposuction on my face so it wouldn't look so round and fat. By health standards, I was extremely fit – I had a private track and field coach, I held records for my times in the 100 metre sprint, I was simultaneously in ballet, and had the muscular build to match all my activities. On paper I had everything going for me and still I purposely avoided mirrors at all costs because I was fully convinced that I was grossly overweight. My attempt to slip into the coat that would assimilate me into typical privileged white teenage culture, became a suffocating waterfall of fabric, which took years upon years of internal work to combat. At the same time, I was a stranger in the world of black culture, I had no clue about the rappers or celebrities that were popular at the time, slang was and still is a struggle for me to understand, I wasn't allowed to wear "ethnic" hairstyles, and "urban" fashion trends never spoke to me – ultimately, trying to be a hip black kid wasn't a coat that fit me.

As I stated before, coat switching can have positive and negative effects, but just as I have mentioned in other parts of this book, our awareness of our reactions to external stimuli create a condition where we can act from a state of empowered thought, rather than a place of guttural reaction.

---

[30] Polycystic ovary syndrome

[31] According to a 2010 article by Silonie Sachdeva in the *Indian Journal of Dermatology* – hirsutism which is defined as the presence of course hairs in a male-like pattern – is a common condition affecting 5 to 10 percent of women and girls of all ages. In a 2006 study published in The Journal of Psychosomatic Research, researchers found that women with unwanted facial hair spent a considerable amount of time checking their facial hair and attempting to remove it, in addition, while most subjects were able to maintain a generally content existence, they frequently struggled with clinical depression, anxiety, and had issues with social relationships.

It took a long time for me to find a comfortable place in my life where coat switching was greatly minimised. I find myself as my friends would say, "Abandoning a coat to check people's privilege…" and the older I get the more, I find myself abandoning the expectation of silent propriety to speak out against injustice or present my opinion about a subject in a rational manner. I absolutely hate confrontational disputes, but I love the art of debate and the civil exchange of ideals.

Not so long ago I attended a music festival where there was a panel discussion about the present buzz word in academic music these days… diversity. This particular festival was quite interesting for me because it was one of the few times that I had participated in an extended event without ties to the logistics of running things. A simple comment was made about how few black people are into classical music and that one might never know why that was — before I could stop myself the soapbox train let the words "Actually, it is a socioeconomic problem caused by systemic racism…" fall out of my mouth. The thing about the soapbox train, is that once I get on it, no matter how uncomfortable I may feel about moving forward with checking someone's or an entire group's privilege, there's no stopping a word train that has an engine so rooted in an articulate painting of social justice issues.

An even more recent event occurred at a middle school. Due to school choice programs and a push for neighbourhood schools, to alleviate bussing and other resource issues, Pinellas County Schools are largely homogeneous in race, with historically black and impoverished communities suffering the most as the children carry gang and neighbourhood problems into the classroom making behavioural concerns and modifications taking extensive time out of actual instruction hours. I firmly believe that it is important for black youth, and particularly black femme youth, to see a strong black woman living and working outside of the paradigms that have been embedded in their psyche for most of their formative years. To this end, I make a point of presenting experimental music workshops for K-12 students throughout the United States.

I visited a middle school theatre class that was primarily full of young black girls, who were studying sound design for theatre at the time of my visit. I focused on introducing the students to my boutique and analog synthesisers, and how one could create foley as well as atmospheric sounds with them. As I turned my back towards the students, so that I could face my performance table and demonstrate how one could create ambient music with the setup that I had brought… several of the girls shouted out "…yeah, but can you make a beat?" I wheeled around quickly in my "NOT TODAY SATAN" shirt and said, "Sure, I can make a beat. The moment I step on stage as a black woman people expect me to make a beat, but I would prefer to subvert expectations…" from there I was on a roll – this time checking the privilege of children and subsequently introducing them to the idea that they are not bound to the societal expectations of "blackness" and we don't need to make music with "beatz." After receiving around of unexpected applause from the students, I allowed the students to come up and interact with my semi-modular electronics, I watched as they tentatively began exploring what happened when they changed patch points or turned knobs… I let them know that there are no mistakes when exploring with electronic music, only happy accidents.

When I walked away from the school, I saw a group of young girls who had been empowered, who were open to questioning the expected path. I don't expect any child or adult who attends one of my workshops to come away with a thirst for a career in experimental music, that has never been my goal and I think that arts education programs sometimes put too much pressure on children to move towards set careers in the arts – my purpose on this planet is to inspire people to question what they believe, to question how they act, and to empower them to take action to improve their circumstances so that just like standing resonant waves that build upon each other and morph into a tidal wave of sound – a tidal wave of kindness and love for this extraordinary experience we call life can be felt profoundly throughout the world.

By my mum's standards, she feels that I'm too American – which translates as too open about my personal affairs. In truth, I actually maintain a fair share of walls and boundaries. Even though I have become more outspoken about social justice issues that primarily stem from my passion for building a world in which there's equity, inclusion, and opportunities unity for all; I am very guarded about my personal life. I share a ton of stories about fun and interesting things that I have done or seen, I make people laugh, and I inspire them to think – but the things in my heart, the things that I hold close to my chest, those are things that dwell behind a series of well-constructed walls.

The older I get, the more I seem to fortify my walls – I am open to using my experiences to help others, but when it comes to vulnerability of my heart, you might as well be trying to pillage Fort Knox. We use the term friend to commonly in our society, and as you delve into what makes you feel the most fulfilled in Platonic relationships, you will find that not everyone is capable of the things that you need or fully receptive of the things that you are able to give from your heart. It is because every human comes to the table with a different set of inherent traits and has been forged by different trials of fire, that I absolutely hate the term "best friend" because it devalues the people who are giving you the 100% that they have, which may be only 20% of your expectations. Being humans we start filing people in categories based on our interactive history with them or people that had similar traits. I have a new set of lookouts on my north tower ready to spot anyone who remotely resembles the man who was the source of my first gaslighting experience. I have another set of guards on my wall for people akin to combrosers[32] who used me to further their own careers.

In a time when we are trying to break down walls, why would I advocate having some? You need walls to guard your heart; however, you can guard your heart without turning into a cold being. Just because you aren't letting people past the castle gates to touch the crown jewels, does not mean you are unable or unwilling to meet them at the border of your lands, to offer them resources or assistance on their journeys. It doesn't mean the traveller that you meet on the road is completely barred from entering your fortress, it just means that you are more careful with who comes through your doors. In a contemporary example, my mum's British heritage means that it is an honour to be invited into one's home, because your domicile is a sacred place of privacy, and it takes several meetings to build up the rapport to be invited in further than the parlour.

---

[32] Combrosers is a new term, created to describe a collection of composers, who do not apologise for their sexist or racist behaviour, or purport to be an ally of the oppressed while simultaneously and selfishly exploiting disenfranchised populations for their own career benefits.

Steven Head is the most understated person one could ever meet. He has talents in spades, strength and gentleness wrapped in one package, but the thing that has always captivated me about Steven is his mind. He is without a doubt one of the most intelligent and probing thinkers that I have in my life. He wins an award for being able to keep my intrigue and attention for literal years. I remember meeting Steven back when I was heavily involved in the noise and experimental music scene in Florida as I was finishing up at Florida Southern College. From the first time I met Steven, I was curious about him and observed him from afar, too afraid to get close to the flame, lest I get burned.

The DIY experimental music and noise music world is not one known for a strong female presence or multicultural participation, particularly in the landscape of Florida underground circa 2008-2011. There is an undercurrent that makes one perpetually feel as though they don't belong. To survive you quickly start assembling a mental list of the people that you feel safe around. Steven has steadily had a place on my list, but I can't say that we grew close through conversation over several years – rather my knowledge of Steven came by musical means, playing with him in various projects here and there throughout the years. When I decided to remove myself from the experimental music scene because I felt that I had no one to trust after Judas betrayed me and began to malign my name; Steven had also, withdrawn from the drama that was going on, and so for a period of a few years we didn't see each other or talk.

One day, my dear friend Jim Ivy approached me about performing in a new project he had that was to premiere on a new series at an Orlando gallery, curated by our mutual friend Patrick Greene. It is about a two and a half hour drive from my place in Saint Petersburg to Orlando, so Jim came by my place earlier in the month to do a rehearsal with me separate from the large rehearsal that he'd had with all of the Orlando-based artists. This first iteration of Tangled Bell included a massive ensemble of artists from a variety of different genres with me as a veritable linchpin that had experience in all the worlds. The original instrumentation had guitar, strings, narration, saxophones, horns, piano, voice, accordion, and drums – just to name a few. It wasn't until I walked into the gallery for the show and Jim directed Steven to sit next to me in the round that I had seen him in at least three years.

There are friends that most people have, who live in far away places and only see on rare occasion; yet, when these kindred souls are reunited, it is as if no time has passed and their rapport is unscathed. This comfort is akin to how I feel with certain collaborators… it just works, and more than just working, it feels right.

I will admit that when it comes to ensemble rehearsals, I often battle extreme self-confidence and perfectionist issues. Thanks to some bad experiences with rehearsals in NYC during my career, I am completely aware of the concept that everyone is replaceable contingent on their performance during the rehearsal process. There was one gig in NYC that I had where the composer removed me from her piece, literally twenty-four hours before the concert. I don't recall looking at Steven more than two or three times during that first performance of Tangled Bell, I was completely at ease musically, but something energy-wise was different, this was a new Steven and I wasn't quite sure what to do with the curiosity and intrigue that he was unwittingly fostering in my mind.

Our shared love of music and mutual respect for each other are what binds us together. My instincts were right, there was an energy shift happening within Steven and it lead to one day where he actually opened up to me about his thoughts and feelings about life. There are things that we don't talk about, things that I understand because empathy and instinct make them clear to me, but I now live in a paradigm where I fiercely want to see Steven succeed and be happy in life, while simultaneously wanting to share pieces of my world with him. In Steven letting down his wall, an incredible thing happened – my heart softened.

I like to tour because I enjoy independence, I love a challenge, I am humbled by sharing my art with others, I enjoy embracing new cultures and people; but most of all, I love that I don't have to concern myself with the people and things back home. The older I get, the less I have a desire to maintain a connection with anyone other than my parents when I am on the road… or rather that is the way it used to be. If you want a chance to touch my heart, give me a good playlist for the road.

Cornelius – *Mellow Waves (2017)* – a suggestion that literally changed my life. I was about to head out on the road again and Steven suggested this album, I remember melting into the sonic world within the first ten-seconds, from then on I listened on repeat, turning each moment of the album over in my mind. Suddenly, I found myself wanting to discuss the album with Steven between breaks in my schedule, and remarkably, I wanted to know how he was doing back home. The latter was interesting to me since I do periodically talk to friends or family on the road, but the general rule is don't saddle me with anything heavy while I am away and working. However, in this case I wanted to hear the good and the bad, I wanted to be a comfort even though I was thousands of miles away.

A new world was emerging, one where I realised that while I don't need to take on the burdens of home, but I can still be empathetic and find ways to surprise the people I care about from the road. I enjoy finding small things on tour that I know he will enjoy or sending notes of encouragement in the mail to Steven. From the practice of sending little notes, came a flooding resurgence of my love of writing old-fashioned handwritten letters to friends, family, and colleagues across the globe. A heart that was closed to love for protection, now allows dulcet tones to travel over the walls and letters from far off lands to cycle from door to door.

At the same time my heart was opening on a personal level for Steven, I was about to be reminded why I have walls in the first place. It started with an email, and an inquiry about my nonprofit, when I met him he had an eerie resemblance to Judas, which should have been my cue to stay away. Ethan was the very definition of a combroser, a man who dances on or crosses the line with women to further his career, while simultaneously purporting to carry the flag for women's rights. The art world is a very interesting place to navigate when it comes to relationships, particularly because so much of our identities and emotions are linked to our professional expression. It is for this reason, that I like clear boundaries and honesty. We are all adults, don't talk to me for hours and hours on end for six months in a flirtatious manner without telling me that you have a girlfriend. I will never understand the mass amount of artists and people in general, that have issues with just telling the truth. We are adults. I can't solve a problem or give you the correct guidance if you provide me with false information.

In the continuation of giving a second chance to people who have made mistakes or otherwise deceived me, I gave Ethan another chance and we started a duo together. We made music and played gigs together, and I even came to care for the live-in girlfriend that he had neglected to introduce me to or even mention for the first six months of our acquaintanceship.

My professional walls are simple and clear cut. When I am on the road, I am working and we treat it like the job that it is, that means we don't get drunk, we don't get high, we don't divulge personal information, and we try to maintain proper decorum at all times. Substance abuse is something that Elizabeth is not here to condone. It is a cheque that I cannot and will not cosign, so when Ethan drank "lost count how many beers" before a gig in Asheville while on tour with me, I was full of emotions and felt wholly unsafe as well as disappointed. Many cues in ensemble musical performance are non-verbal cues. Attempting to communicate with drunk people on a verbal level is already less than fruitful, and attempting to communicate with them on a non-verbal level is next to impossible. I am usually able to subvert my anger and trade it in for something positive, but I was never so angry during a performance when Ethan missed all my cues, drank on stage, hit my bass so hard that it got damaged, and caused our set to run thirty minutes over the allotted time. I felt simultaneously betrayed and isolated in a single set.

I am the sort of person, that tries to stuff my anger and manage it rather than exploding the world. On a quiet drive from Asheville to Athens, Ethan tried to pull the matter out of me, and I explained that in my life I have not been able to trust people who drink to excess and I was made very uncomfortable by his actions the previous evening. He told me that he wouldn't do it again and that in the future, if I was uncomfortable just tell him and he would stop the behaviour. On the surface, that seems like a reasonable resolution to the issues at hand… except, by the time behaviour has escalated to the point where one is forced into expressing their discomfort with the situation, one is far past the point of reasoning with someone who has ingested substances that alter their state of mind. It was at this point that I started to notice that Ethan was drinking every moment that he could, and at an academic conference just a month later, he had brought a bottle of beer in his backpack to drink before our set. Yet again, I was on a stage conducting a disconnected conversation with a person who was supposed to be a teammate. At that point, I was pleased that I had not let him any further than the inner gates of the fortress, because one month later in Austin, TX, I called him to inform him that I wanted a break from working with him indefinitely – the month after that, I retooled my final performance with him due to illness, so that I could participate remotely, only to find out later from credible sources that he didn't so much as even mention my name, rather using the opportunity to further his solo name – typical combroser move. Due to the well constructed professional walls I'd built up, the removal of Ethan from my life was totally seamless, and to be quite frank, less than a year after all the lies and substance issues – I barely think of him.

As we move further away from an industrial era society where subordinate factory workers never interacted with bosses outside of their jobs, where social media and creative working processes force interaction with co-workers on a regular basis – we need walls to protect us from possible harm mentally and emotionally. Professional barriers are also, key when considering the commonality of workplace romances, in such a scenario the presence of workplace walls saves other co-workers from awkward moments and increases overall efficiency and productivity.

Every workplace has a share of inter-office drama and the art world is no different with a laundry list of love stories, broken hearts, betrayal, and affairs. It is an unreasonable expectation for people with the extra ordinary passion and sensitivity paramount to the artistic identity, to extricate themselves from the strong emotions that are tied to the process of art-making.

"Did you hear about what happened with [insert names here] and how they [insert gossip here]?"

"No, I was practicing."

The exchange above is how most of my career in music school played out. I wasn't around for most of the dramatic things and intrigue in the department because I was doing my job as a student, which was practicing. It continues to be a model for how my professional working life pans out. Generally, I don't go out to the bar with people after rehearsals or shows, and if I do go out I'm ordering a Shirley Temple with extra cherries.

Professional musicians and music educators are some of the most intense partiers that I have ever met. The things that happen at music educators conferences, where people are posted up in hotels with per diems often paid by taxpayers dollars are in a sense deplorable. Yes, everyone needs to and wants to unwind, but that doesn't mean that they need to drink to excess, and alcohol never excuses bad behaviour.

On the flip side, music festivals are a hot bed for inappropriate behaviour and unethical exploits. Even if consenting adults of legal age are involved, there's something very dirty and problematic about people engaging in physical exploits when one or more of the parties is in a position of power. The #MeToo movement brought to the forefront a lot of issues with regard to sexual harassment and oppressive workplace structures, but the fact that a superior can have casual drunken relations with a subordinate and nobody turns a blind eye is also, problematic because even though the involved parties are consenting adults the behaviour is still unethical.

Having a professional wall that precludes me from spending time around my drunken colleagues has not effected my career in any negative manner. People often believe that deals in the art world are made over drinks and "networking" over cocktails. I say, you can easily make an appointment for coffee or to chat over Skype about potential projects – one important thing I learned from my boss when I was working as a legislative researcher for an administrative consulting attorney, is that any agreement made over alcohol can be argued as null and void because one of the parties might not have met the legal capacity as defined in basic principles of contract law to enter into the agreement – the measure of my worth is not defined by how well I can consume alcohol and lose track of my inhibitions.

Dearest reader, the measure of your professional worth and merit is not defined by your ability to party. I can safely say, that the best deals I have ever made were negotiated without the presence of substances [33] and I have never felt that I missed out on an opportunity because I decided to go to bed instead of out to a bar.

I am a big fan of pieces of paper and time-stamped evidence. Working with artists is rarely a straightforward path, especially when you are dealing with inexperienced individuals who lack self-confidence in their work or the project at hand. Early in my career, I shied away from doling out contracts for every gig because I was working with friends and didn't want to complicate relationships, now as an established artist, I rarely enter into a project without a written contract. I have been screwed over the most by people who call themselves my friends, and these are the "collaborations" in which I've often felt the most artistically stifled if I don't have a contract in place.

Everyone has their own process to creation, and it is not fair for another party to impose their belief system on another human being under regular circumstances, and definitely not okay to encroach upon the safe space a creative has fostered for productivity. It is unethical to ask someone else to engage in prayer or rituals. It is unethical to ask for benefits of an intimate nature. It is unethical to encroach on the safety of someone else's personal process without express invitation from said individual.

When I was in community college in Saint Petersburg, my piano lessons and ethics classes were in the same building. Still in the main entrance to the building today, and I often think of the accuracy of it's foreshadowing, is a sign that says Fine Arts one way and Ethics the other way. So many people at all levels of the entertainment industry in all areas including academic, religious, secular, and more encounter ethical dilemmas on a regular basis. The main problem with being an artist and freelance contractor, is that you don't have a Human Resources Department to step in when you witness a veritable orgy happening between a faculty member at a festival and their students or subordinates. To whom do you complain when you are constantly

---

[33] Other than the large amounts of caffeine in my regular cup of Kyoto drip from Bandit Coffee Co.

hassled by someone about faith-based practices as a part of your artistic process? You don't have an advocate in your court — but you have a piece of paper that set down guidelines and consequences and ultimately boundaries to protect you.

Walls, also keep the plague of doubt from spreading. I have a love-hate relationship with collaboration. I detest people who use collaboration for personal gains and ride on the coattails of others. I love collaboration when it causes both individuals to grow and evolve into better people and ultimately better artists. I have had a number of collaborators who were really just using me as a stepping stone for their careers, because they lacked their own legitimacy without my name. However, it isn't the hanger-on and deceitful collaborators that irritate me the most; no, that honour is reserved for the people who allow their insecurities to infect other people involved in the production process. The neediest clients I have ever had to deal with are the ones who only have a few projects to their name, they call me at all hours of the day and night to talk about their fears and what they wish I could do and it is emotionally exhausting for me to handle. Insecurity often manifests in a manner where the leader of the project ends up micromanaging a situation to the point that other artists involved feel completely stifled. People who lack confidence within themselves and try to elicit power over others discreetly through microaggressions are also problematic to overall productivity.

In one of my various jobs over the years, I composed for a local fledgling dance company, and I was paid far less than a living wage for hours and hours of work. A composer's job does not end at the studio door, it just begins and we spend hours upon hours in our home studios to create scores to be used by choreographers. When I was tied to the dance company, I felt trapped, I felt as though I couldn't breathe artistically. What started as seemingly great collaboration, quickly escalated into requests for me to just copy music off of Spotify, and a choreographer who demanded that I have the score done by first rehearsal but never choreographed to my music or even listened to it before hand. Beyond that, there was an executive director who instead of mediating issues, sat back and did nothing or stirred the pot and allowed things to explode. I have rarely felt so irritated or humiliated as when I spoke with a choreographer the day before a rehearsal, explained my concept, worked until the early hours of the morning, then came into company rehearsal to find she hadn't listened to the piece, and hadn't listened to what I had said about the work the day before, and subsequently insulted my work in front of a new company member while the executive director sat idly by and did nothing. For a long time, I felt powerless to this sort passive aggressive control structure abound with microaggressions, but then I decided to take action – though messy, I severed my ties completely with the individuals that weren't treating my art with the respect it deserved. To protect myself from falling into similar situations in the future, I decided to add verbiage to all of my commission contracts which states I will charge extra for each additional major edit that a client requests.

Setting up clearly defined walls protects you, but it also clearly defines your worth. In business, walls are the foundation of a strong prosperous career with quick recovery from shots fired by rogue individuals. In your personal life, walls foster healthy self-care habits and guard your heart from careless mistakes that can have long-term repercussions.

WALLS & COAT SWITCHING
NETWORKING & SOCIALISING SURVIVAL TACTICS
REFLECTION & GUIDED SELF-ASSESSMENT QUESTIONS

What are the coats that you wear based on the group or situation in which you frequently find yourself?

_____
_____
_____
_____
_____
_____
_____
_____
_____
_____

What are some positive aspects of the coats you frequently wear?

_____
_____
_____
_____
_____
_____
_____

What are some negative aspects of the various coats that you wear?

How can you move to injecting more of your authentic self into situations where coat-switching many be necessary to survival?

How can you create an informed positive space that invites the individuals with whom you interact for work to be the most authentic versions of themselves?

How can you create an informed positive space that invites the individuals with whom you interact in your personal and social life to be the most authentic versions of themselves?

What do the walls that guard your heart look like?

What are the weak points of your personal fortress?

Think about your present and ideal working environments. Define the boundaries that not only make you feel comfortable enough to do your job, but also promote maximum efficiency.

Considering your boundaries, how can you effectively enforce them in a professional manner, and what consequence structure can you set up to deal with or otherwise deter people from crossing your lines without consent?

NOT MEANT FOR ME
LEARNING TO COPE WITH REJECTION

I wake up to rejection emails on a regular basis. As a working artist, I apply to a lot of opportunities including calls for scores, calls for proposals, artist residency programs, music festivals, arts organisations, grant programs, appeal to other performers, and send out emails to various contacts to plan my own tours. If you are in an arts program, you are likely to have experience with critiques in studio classes. Andraya introduced me to the world of visual arts critiques through her graphic design core classes and studio art electives, I learned how to talk about art outside of my own medium, which is a skill that has greatly assisted me with interdisciplinary collaborations in my professional life. As the only classical guitar performance major, my studio classes were a bit of tag team critiques from both of my guitar professors, and I had to eat a lot of things from praise to rejection. In studio, mixing, and ensemble classes for my commercial music production studies almost every meeting was about analysing, clearly articulating, and backing up your critique with evidence. I learned quickly, that not everyone is going to have the same tastes or interpretations of a work as another person; within a single population there are many different versions of hearing and absorption of material. All of these experiences over my formative artistic years numbed the sting of rejection within my professional world, but it took a while to synthesise these lessons into my personal reality. Rejection is in this way akin to immunotherapy, graduated introduction of a substance to which one has an adverse reaction ultimately leads the body to building up a tolerance to an allergen or in laboratory studies – cancer.[34]

When we feel unhappy or unstable with our present state of affairs at any given point of our lives, we start to fixate on particular opportunities as a means to escape. We are driven by consumption and an insatiable thirst for the next big opportunity, while such an unquenchable fire can lead us to create some amazing things, it can also lead us to making

---

[34] Immunotherapy is still new in the world of cancer treatment but works on the basis of strengthening the power of the bodies own white cells, so that they are strong enough to attach cancer cells the same way they attack viruses, bacteria, and allergens.

decisions from a places of desperation as opposed to ones of informed empowerment.

The worst collaborations and opportunities that I have ever been apart of are the ones that were forced. Around 2016, I came back from a stint of solo touring seeking a way back into my local community. I was at a crossroads where I was feeling increasingly isolated with every return from the road, and I thought that perhaps collaborating with others would bring me back into feeling connected to my hometown. The commonality between all these incidents of forced collaboration is that I was not living up to my best artistic standards.

Two of the major incidents where I was forced to collaborate with others were spurred on from pressure by local arts organisations. In one particular instance, I essentially cried to an executive director, and told her I wanted to be released from the contract that bound me to toxic individuals. I was told that it would make everyone look bad, if I pulled out of the project.[35] Over the next several months, I received harassing emails from one of the collaborators, and this individual met with community leaders behind my back to malign my name. A direct result of this forced collaboration was me removing myself from the nonprofit sector completely and ending an organisation that had done a lot of work for the community over the course of almost five years.

After I ended my nonprofit work and removed myself from participating in the local arts community, so that I could avoid people who were sending harassing correspondence my way and because I was completely cognisant that my career was never confined to the boundaries of Pinellas County; I was asked by two arts organisations to participate in their fall events. At the first I had wonderful musical collaborators, but an audience that literally laughed at my composition. Amidst the swirling cackles, even though the work was up to par and inline with the concept-driven artistic voice that marks the mature portion of my career, I was taken back to my final months at Florida Southern College, where I was just beginning to experiment with *music*

---

[35] In hindsight, this was a manipulative comment because I the project had nothing to do with my personal professional career, which by that time was well established; rather, it was the attachment of my name to the project that raised the optics of emerging artists tied to the project.

concrète[36] and heard a sea of laughter from classmates who had no understanding of experimental work, even though it was a topic discussed in our mandatory music history classes. Within the same week, I was arranging a sound installation at a local gallery for a fundraiser, when one of the organisation employees damaged a portion of my work, when tripping over a speaker that had yet to be gaffed into place. I felt disrespected when the same executive director that had only a year ago forced me to work with people that ultimately were so toxic that there was discussion about whether or not I should file an order of protection; made me eat the cost and effort of finding replacement units. I was also, irritated because on principle if a gallery damages a visual artist's work, they don't just hang the painting back on the wall with a hole in it. Galleries have insurance for exhibitions to make sure that in their stewardship of the art, they have a safety net to repair any portion of a damaged work. The fact that the same care was not shown for a sound artist, was a level of disregard that left me seriously questioning whether or not I could ever work in the community again on an artistic level.

What keeps me coming back for more metaphorical punches in the face, is the constant thought in the back of my mind that every battle I fight, is one less battle for the little brown girls coming up behind me in my field. Every person that I have worked with that has sent harassing emails meant to denigrate me and my abilities, has also been obsessed with putting their name on everything and taking a huge centre spotlight. Individuals who are secure in their identities, confident in their abilities, who view their work as an artist as a professional vocation and calling – are people who tend to have no regard for the spotlight outside of the functional recognition that it is a part of their job. I don't need to prove myself. At thirty years old, I have an extensive and wide-reaching body of work that speaks for itself. I concern myself with constant evolution of my artistic voices and personal being because I don't feel that I have expressed everything that I was placed on this Earth to explore through my lens of perception; but a large portion of my focus outside of my practice, is about finding and empowering the voices of potential and emerging talent or at the very least creating a platform for their work to be seen and respected.

---

[36] *Music concrète* is a form of early experimental music where collections of tape samples were spliced, and modified by a composer to create a fixed media work.

You don't have to be in the limelight to have an impact on others. When I am home, I love to be a hermit and get everything possible delivered to my house. I also, LOVE sushi burritos, and this results in me ordering in probably more than my certified financial planner James Cioccia, Jr., would advise me to do throughout a calendar year. In the little spot where you can leave special instructions for the kitchen, I always make sure to thank the people at Pacific Counter for their work and let them know how much I appreciate them. In turn, I'm surprised every time they send me a kind note on my paper bag or biodegradable food container. There are several colleagues, for whom I have written biographies, assisted with technical questions, career advice, and proposal writing. I have never asked them for renumeration for these consultation services, but when they succeed and rise to more public notoriety, I am fulfilled knowing that I had a hand in their success. Because a lot of the people that I mentor are in the same or similar field as me, there are a great deal of opportunities that I could apply for in opposition to my mentees and would likely get because I have more experience to my name; instead of hoarding the opportunities for myself, I frequently share that information with others, including peers with similar background experience.

There's enough space for everyone to succeed in this world, but if you hoard all the opportunities, you create a market of scarcity and desperation that results in a typhoon of bad decisions. If you are meant to have a specific opportunity, it will happen, and sometimes you have to keep applying because the timing just isn't right.

Rejection is a healthy part of life, and from a professional standpoint it gives us a lot of information to reevaluate our practice.[37] When an artist is working in their studio or collaborating with others, the lens of their work is largely measured by their personal yardstick or validated peers that have extensive knowledge of their work and the source history from which is emanates. When one takes the opportunity to apply to a grant program or other public opportunity, suddenly new eyes are on the body of one's work; moreover, one is often required to summarise

---

[37] I publicly speak about the revising our view of rejection on a regular basis, and a guest post I wrote for Creative Pinellas during my time as an Individual Artist Grantee *The Importance of Rejection* included in Appendix A.

their practice in a concise manner. The creation and execution of your ideas whether artistic or purely entrepreneurial in nature is only one half of the equation – you have to know how to speak about who you are and how you define your work, otherwise others will categorise you as they see fit.[38]

The golden thread we have uncovered as we have worked through this book, is that in order to have a resonant life, one must be empowered, which comes from being master of your own destiny and your own definition. When you allow others to construct a summary of your life and being, you give them the power. It is incredibly difficult to rewrite a narrative that other people have spread like wildfire. Alternatively, if you start off with a clear vision of who you are and enforce that vision, any rejection that comes your way can be dealt with in a constructive manner because it is not based on hearsay or clouded by feelings.

To make the most of rejection, one must remove their ego from the equation. One of my father's training manuals for salespeople states primary reasons that people fail to close a deal or even interest a client into initial conversation come because – the salesperson has not explained the product well-enough, the client doesn't understand the need for the product, or the approach came at the wrong time. Notice that none of the mentioned explanations say anything about the product being subpar or flawed. As an artist or entrepreneur often rejection comes from an error in the attempt to present one's work, not because the artwork is less than stellar.[39] Sometimes you are appealing to the wrong audience, and other times you have to explain to the client or other party why your idea or product is needed, and sometimes that means you have to poke holes to expose an overlooked portion of their operations. When you can demonstrate that a client actually does have a marked need for what you are offering, their tune usually changes.

When we release ourselves from the mindset that rejection is a sign of some larger flaw within our beings, and instead embrace that it is a

---

[38] See *PLEASE DON'T CALL ME A COMPOSER, CLASSICAL MUSICIAN, TOY PIANIST… in Appendix A for the original where I publicly defined and labeled myself as. New Renaissance Artist.*

[39] Sometimes one does need to go back to the drawing board and reevaluate their process; however, as an established artist this is rarely the case because one is resolute in their voice and technique by this time.

natural part of the world that shifts as much as the trade winds, we are able to weather the storms of rejection, gauge the direction of the winds, and reset our course of action. When we release our claws of expectation from opportunities that have eluded us, we are free to put our energy and efforts into new prospects. When we realise that there are other people in this world deserving of opportunities, and that sometimes our rejection is necessary to make way for the people behind us on the rope bridge, it becomes easier to let others pass. Do not allow jealousy or pangs of self-doubt to blackout the dazzling passionate fire within your being.

NOT MEANT FOR ME
LEARNING TO COPE WITH REJECTION

REFLECTION & GUIDED SELF-ASSESSMENT QUESTIONS

Are you the type of person that holds on tightly to rejection? Why do you think it is difficult for you to let go?

_____

_____

_____

_____

_____

_____

_____

_____

_____

_____

_____

_____

_____

_____

_____

_____

_____

_____

_____

Do you stay in situations longer than you should, because you fear rejection? Identify some specific examples.

Do you find yourself obsessing over opportunities that you didn't get or people that didn't meet your relationship expectations? Identify some specific examples.

What can you glean about how you others are interpreting the manner in which you present yourself and your work from past rejections?

If you feel that there is a miscommunication about how you perceive yourself and your work that is contributing to rejection of your ideas, how can you clarify and define yourself in a manner that leaves no room for people to mis-categorise you based on their own experience or prejudice?

RESONATE

WE CARRY OUR HOMES WITHIN US
THE LITTLE THINGS & OUR MENTAL PHOTO ALBUM

When you live out of a suitcase for most of the year, you learn to live as a minimalist. Airlines only allow so much luggage without charging astronomical fees, you have to carry all the things you bring on the road with you, and as discussed in earlier chapters, one must be hyper vigilant about every piece of property with which they travel. When you in essence, work over twenty hours a day, you have little time to think about picking up your phone to scroll through memories in your photo album; additionally, you often need to save storage for photos and video that can be used for marketing purposes.

When no physical place is exactly home, you start to realise that your home is stored in the sweet and funny memories that you share with specific people. When you are not bound by ties to a physical place, it makes a nomadic life emotionally possible. This last chapter focuses on some of the delightful memories that I often look to on the road, to remind me of the people that make my existence feel meaningful. These are the stories of mundane and normal that remind me of my humanity and value beyond my artistic contributions to the world.

A Quest for Pizza
There aren't many women on the engineering side of music, and while being one of less than ten in an entire music production program led to the beginning of my friendship with Keirsten Johnson[40], there's much more that binds us together. We played music together in a jazz fusion group during college, and earned extra money from performing for museum exhibition openings, with me on piano and Keirsten on electric bass. We have been there for each other at our best and our worst. We support each other, but aren't afraid to call one another out on foolish ideas or nonsense. We don't have to speak every day, but when we get together it is as if no time has passed between us.

---

[40] Also, Keirsten and my cousin Conrhonda look like twins separated at birth. The first time that I actually introduced myself to Keirsten in the school hallway, it was because she was essentially a doppelgänger for my favourite cousin. While it happened a ton when we were in school, even today when we go places together people regularly mistake Keirsten and I for blood related sisters.

I am highly adaptable; however, there are few people that I can actually travel with, let alone share a hotel and a few solid days with – I need space and time to rejuvenate, which often that looks like my travel companion sitting in silence with me while I work on something, read, or just stare off into the distance pondering the meaning of life. Keirsten has always had a knack for understanding when I need space, but still want company, and this is why she is on the top of the list of people with whom I would willingly travel for an extended period of time.

In 2013, I was considering going off to school in California, and I had a scholarship audition at Mills College in Oakland, CA. I had previously visited the Bay Area on a school-sponsored trip to the Audio Engineering Society Convention and was super excited about introducing Keirsten to some of my favourite places in the area. I was additionally excited about the prospect of attending the same school as my beloved audio mentor Dave Greenberg.

I left from the Orlando International Airport on United Airlines the same day as Keirsten two hours after she left Tampa International Airport traveling on Southwest Airlines. Somehow, I arrived about one hour before Keirsten at San Francisco International Airport. By the time that we got on the BART and to our hotel, it was about midnight. We were staying in a considerably humble hotel as compared to the fancy Palace Hotel that I had stayed in on my school-sponsored AES Convention visit.

After traveling for such a long time, we were both tired and hungry. This section of the city outside of the Financial District was new to me, and so I didn't have a solid idea of a late night place to get to on foot. We asked the friendly front desk man who told us "in good conscience" he could not advise us to turn left, rather directing us to turn right at the end of the block and follow the path until we would eventually happen upon a burger joint like Hardee's. Well, we set out on foot into the darkness, unaware of how far we needed to walk, with cellphones that were too low on battery power to use GPS – the adventure had begun.

San Francisco has a notorious problem with homelessness and drug abuse, my mentor has always said that the best way to turn down drugs in the Bay Area is to just tell them you do a harder drug. Keirsten and I were armed with this knowledge as we ambled with haste along the cool night streets. As we crossed over the first darkened city block we were approached unexpectedly by a dishevelled duo who were purporting to sell copies of The Homeless Newspaper – which sparks so many questions – Why are we giving the homeless access to a printing press, but not investing that money in housing and rehabilitation resources for the people living on the streets?

As we continued on the seemingly never ending path to the burger joint we came to the first street corner bathed in light, it featured an abandoned building, sex shops, and a club that was just letting out. We looked down the street to the right and saw a local pizza place. Mutually decided in a look that we were going to take our chances on the pizza spot. On our way we encountered a gaunt and winkled old black woman, clearly hardened by the streets – she offered us crack-cocaine and we politely told her "No thanks, we only do heroin." She responded with a simple "That's straight," and left us to our own devices, we continued on our excursion… towards questionable pizza. We safely made it into the pizza place and ordered a whole pie and a Sierra Mist to split. We looked up to find the same woman from just up the street, stiffly dancing in pizza shop doorway with a boombox the clearly broken, missing the cover for the CD compartment, with no batteries, and completely silent. About only ten minutes had elapsed since we saw her on the street, and I had so many questions like "where she obtained this device in the short time between her offering us drugs and us ordering pizza?" And just as I was musing on these universal questions, Keirsten interrupted in a shady whisper meant only for my ears… "cocaine is a hell of a drug."

Celebration within the mundane
I have mentioned my dear friend Andraya, in other sections of this book, but I include this one particular memory here because life is not measured in value but the "big moments" and CV building achievements.

While Andraya has always supported me in my life, I have always been her cheerleader as well. I was so happy when she found her longtime partner Krystal, and I was even happier when they announced that they were getting a house together. I was so honoured when they invited me to be their first house guest after I came back from an extended tour. At the time of my visit, they were still moving into the house and so we decided on something simple – breakfast for dinner. I recall that the mixer had yet to be unpacked, so Andraya made the waffle batter in the blender. As Krystal opened the cabinet to get seasoning for the eggs, I looked up to the top shelf and saw rainbow sprinkles. My eyes grew big with excitement akin to ta child seeing their favourite storybook character in real life, "Are those rainbow sprinkles, and can we use them in the waffles?" Both Krystal and Andraya happily agreed, and as Andraya started making the batter she tentatively added coloured sugar sprinkles… that is until she opened the lid of the blender and declared there wasn't enough rainbow and proceeded to add about half of the bottle of sprinkles. We sat down to the table and had the first Funfetti Waffle Friday.

A well-coordinated surprise
If you haven't figured it out by this point in the book, I'll make it crystal clear now, I show my love for people through sharing my time with them in the midst of busy schedules. I love to surprise friends who think that I can't attend an event by showing up unexpectedly to support them. In the summer of 2015, I was slated to play at the triennial Delta Omicron conference in Illinois, and at the same time my dear friends Nathan, Leo, Laith, and Danny were getting ready to go on tour with their bands Nude Tayne and Jitters. The first show of their tour was in Orlando at a DIY space that was probably called The Space Station at the time. I took lots of photos in Chicago and posted my condolences on Facebook about missing the kick-off show, and my plan was in full motion. You see, I had found a deal that allowed me to come into the Orlando International Airport and rent a car from Enterprise, so I could drive to the venue in Orlando and then another two hours back to St. Petersburg. When I pulled up to the venue, I had actually magically arrived before the guys, and while the people at the venue were super gracious, I still feel very uncomfortable in any scene that resembles a party in any form. Soon Leo pulled up with the van and the guys hopped out, in full focus on moving gear mode but equally excited to see me. Blue and red lights in a small warehouse stage, and the humidity of a Floridian summer night… these are the sense memories that I hold. It was also, the first time any of us went to Pom Pom's and the first time I had their delicious vegetarian sandwich and Nathan had their famous Thanksgiving dinner sandwich. It is crazy how certain senses

bind us to certain memories. About a year or so later a Pom Pom's franchise opened up in my hometown of St. Petersburg. I go to the one near my house from time to time, and while I know all of their sandwiches are distinct and different, I have never ordered anything else but their vegetarian sandwich on pumpernickel bread. With Danny constantly on the road, Laith consumed by work, Leo living in a different state on the East coast, and Nathan living clear on the other side of the country – as ridiculous as it sounds, I eat that sandwich in Saint Petersburg, Florida and suddenly I'm transported to lively conversations and killer music on a humid night in humble Orlando.

The One, The Only Jim Ivy

Of all my collaborators in the experimental and noise community, the most upstanding and best fosterer of sonic safe spaces is Jim Ivy. There are few people that I would reorientate my schedule so I could participate in their project these days, but if Jim Ivy asked me to reprise my roles in his works Game Piece or Tangled Bell, I would do so in a heartbeat. When I revealed to Jim the extent to which I felt violated by a particular man in the scene, Jim took it upon himself to confront this individual in person about their behaviour and told them that they needed to make amends. Not many people would have the courage to stand up for women in the manner that Jim did and to this day I am in awe of his strength of character. It is this genuine energy that comes forth when you interact with Jim as an improvisor in a group, but it comes forward even further when you are performing one of his works. The most important lesson I learned from Jim, is that if you have great players and you give them space to do what they do best, your initial vision can evolve beyond your wildest dreams. As a performer, knowing that the conductor/composer/collaborator has complete faith in your abilities leaves space for you to push yourself further and to explore new possibilities within the ensemble network as well as your own practice. In one of the performances of *Tangled Bell*, the violinist, Sarah Morrison and I ended up falling into a neo-romantic duet, a style that both of us had studied in our collegiate instrumental instruction but something that was completely foreign to our natural improvisatory tendencies.

As a performer, I have worked with a lot of composers and felt super constricted by their vision of a human who is expected to perform a work in the same manner that their music notation software has rendered the work – perfect, robotic, void of interpretation. There's even a school of composers that intentionally write things that are beyond the ability of humans to perform because they are interested in exposing the struggle of the performer as part of the work's process. As a performer, works such as this are not fun, they are stressful and demeaning – these works, which are often written by cisgender white men with advanced terminal degrees, further a patriarchal power structure whereby performers are treated like pawns in play for omnipresent white god. What works with Jim, is that he remembers his works are being performed by humans, he respects that each artist comes to the table with a different background; rather than shunning people he seeks common ground and embraces cross-cultural expression. Jim Ivy's loving kindness in music, yields successful results because he remembers that the energy each individual brings to the table is valid and important to the puzzle.

"San Francisco is a city known to riot..."
In October of 2012, after months of lobbying the Student Government Association for funds to send delegates from the recording arts program to the Audio Engineering Society conference in San Francisco, California, I boarded a plane in Tampa and after three tiring legs over the course of eight hours, we all made it to San Francisco. Since I was the most organised and the only woman, I had been left in charge by our advisor to make sure that the hotel and tickets were handled. We were staying at the historic and very expensive Palace Hotel in the heart of the Financial District. I was concerned about getting all of our affairs sorted, but the guys were more interested in getting their hands on a certain green plant that was legal in California but at the time very illegal in our home state of Florida. They were loud raucous, uncouth, and quite frankly my British side took hold and I was angry with embarrassment. My face read such that the kind gentleman at the desk placed six floors between me and the boys. I relegated myself to a different schedule and exploring much of the city on my own, after situating everyone with their hotel key cards and conference passes.

October 2012, was a major year for sports in San Francisco. While we were at the conference, the San Francisco Giants were playing the

Detroit Tigers in the World Series. With a father who played professional football, I have grown to harbour a deep seated disdain for organised sports. I mention this because I wasn't keeping tabs on the games, but my intuition has always been sharp as a tack. The last night we stayed in San Francisco, there was something in the air... I could just tell that this was a night that I wanted to stay in and curl up with a warm meal and go to bed. So I set out to a pizza place in walking distance that was recommended highly by Yelp reviews, as I waited for my pizza, I could feel the energy shifting... I made my way to CVS and purchased some water and soda, my pace quickened with each passing moment as if I was preparing to run away from something. By the time I made it back to the hotel, the boys wanted to come and hang out in my room and watch TV. All of a sudden, there were audible cheers from the street – "GIANTS WIN! GIANTS WIN!" I looked down from the sixth floor window to see people taking to the streets. I said, "We should probably go to our rooms and try to sleep, San Francisco is a city known to riot." "You probably should have listened to Elizabeth," is a phrase that has been uttered too many times to count, and this situation was no different. The boys left my room and I secured all the locks, finished packing, and listened to the chaos unfolding below. A throng that over took the entirety of the streets began chanting "FUCK DETROIT! FUCK DETROIT!" I looked down to see someone who had pulled a ramshackle drum kit into the street and was going to town on it, setting the tempo for the growing hoard of people. Soon fires began to break out, people attempted to tip over a city bus, the hotel was placed on lockdown, police sirens sounded, and the chanting took on a new slogan "FUCK THE POLICE!" Uniformed officers couldn't make their way in and plain clothes cops infiltrated the crowd, using tasers on people at random, and the chaos began to disperse in all directions. I fell asleep soon after in the safety and comfort of my plush hotel bed. I awoke the next day for our 4:00am flight rested and inspired by the white papers presented at the conference I was ready to get back to the East coast and back to work. On the other hand, the guys were dragging and exhausted from participating in the riot. If you ask me, I'll tell you that I totally won, by avoiding the fray of the riot, if you ask the guys they would tell you that it isn't every day that one gets a chance to participate in a riot. If you as our advisor, none of this ever happened, and the boys in no way disgraced or compromised the school with their actions that may or may not have taken place during the riot.

I Don't Want To Talk About It
One of my all time favourite individuals on this planet is Patrick Greene, at double my age, Pat has seen a lot and done a lot. He collects stories and experiences like people collect physical objects. He has a consummate spirit of adventure and will take off on a journey at a moment's notice. One of my favourite stories about Pat is his epic unofficial run for mayor of Orlando, FL. In typical Pat Greene style, his life is art, and his campaign slogan was the soon to be famous and synonymous with Pat, "I don't want to talk about it." When the press reached out to him during his victory party (he didn't actually win) he told them he was sticking to his campaign values and "I don't want to talk about it." For his sixtieth birthday, my friend Christopher Belt wrote a piece for sixty guitars in homage to Glenn Branca's work for one hundred guitarists, and Steven Head managed to wrangle exactly sixty guitarists from near and far to perform this massive tribute to Pat. I don't know anyone else who is so beloved by a local art community or a community in general that could have such a tribute pulled together in just a few short months. Pat is the definition of living a resonant life, while he might not be at the front of everything, he sees lives unapologetically and makes the most of every experience. While Pat is the first one to make mischief, he also follows through on ideas… when I am on the road, I remember that every experience is another story to be told and from which one can learn profound truths of life… at the same time, you are never too old to have fun, to stop taking yourself so seriously, to laugh, to be your authentic self – I thank Pat for creating spaces, and being a role model for life as art and art as life.

Food, Friends, Home, Home On The Road
One of my favourite places to visit on tour is Alabama. Most people think I am absolutely crazy when I say that, but ever since I added Tuscaloosa to my tour route, I've been hooked. I've never played a huge venue in Tuscaloosa, rather all my shows have been intimate ones in the house of my friend Justin Greene. It is curious to see professors from the university alongside students equally engaged in an intimate music experience that I can only compare to the salons of *fin-de-siècle* Paris. The first time I played in Tuscaloosa, Justin was the opening act and he played several pieces for solo glockenspiel that included one where

ping-pong balls were used in lieu of mallets and forced the listener to become acutely aware through the delicacy of the sounds that kissed the air of the performance space. In addition to stellar performances, and an audience that you can feel is hanging on your every drop of concert energy; Justin and his partner Elizabeth Theriot are some of the greatest thinkers I know. I have yet to happen upon an Elizabeth that I don't love, for we are special wonderful people with a strong name, and Elizabeth Theriot is no exception. While Elizabeth is not a classically trained musician, she is an incredible writer, whose words carry their own musicality that draws you in and compels one to feel, to question, and to be moved… her words leave an imprint on your soul. As if it couldn't get any better, Justin is an amazing chef, I rarely get home cooked meals when I am on the road, but I dream all year about the dishes that he has made for me each time I have come to visit. Elizabeth and Justin provide me with a home where I can be my authentic self, where I can grow through discussion of ideas, where I feel safe and nurtured.

When I transferred to Florida Southern College as a junior many years ago, they placed me in the first year girls only dorm with a crop of students fresh out of high school. On my first night, I met Lin Chang who I later found out was in my same department as a music business major. Lin and I would go on to take many classes together in the music program, but our friendship formed from the fact that Lin would always knock on my door in the evenings when she was on rotation for her job as a resident advisor and ask me to hang out or go grab snacks at the campus minimart… to which I would always reply that I was already in my inside pants (pyjama pants) and that I couldn't go outside so underdressed. In any case, I pretty much always relented and then we would knock on Andraya's door and bring her along for the evenings escapades. Today, Lin is based in Nashville, TN and I always try to set aside a day or two in the midst of my tours to visit Lin, unwind, and have lady hangout time. Every visit always ends with a visit to Proper Bagel for fancy bagel sandwiches that I loving refer to as $16 bagels… but we stay up till the wee hours of the morning just talking about life and catching each other up on the things that have gone on, since we last spoke. It is sort of like a grownup version of a slumber party, although we have wine in lieu of jukeboxes. I love to hear about all the things that Lin has been up to and we give each other advice on various life situations. Every moment of my life is somehow connected to my work, I spend most holidays and "free time" thinking about new or existing projects, and there are very few moments in any single year where I shutdown and just focus on being a regular person. When I am with Lin in Nashville, it is all about catching up and eating delicious food and just hanging out. I purposefully, choose to deal with work emails after I leave and remain present in the moment. Home is a lot of things… but when you allow work to invade your home space, you forget what it is like to fully relax and to be present for your friends and loved ones.

Profundity

I started this book with the goal of presenting ways that I have created an existence in this world that is driven by purpose and expands beyond myself to inspire others to question their lives and their realities. As I whittled away at writing the last few chapters of this book, I opened up a simple query to the near wide array of people that I am connected with via social media – *What is the most profound thing that I have ever said to you, or action that I did which has had a positive impact on your life?*

While most of the responses were tailored to specific interactions or events, the common threads were that my words, my openness, my loving kindness, my motivation, and of utmost importance to the majority – the way my performances and art challenged their perception of the world and fostered a new paradigm that regards people and sounds with further care and wonder than previously put forth. If you want to talk about a resonant life… one that reaches beyond your being to touch others and inspire empowered change within themselves, you have to first live a resonant life. I'm not perfect, none of us are perfect, but we can get up each day and make sound waves that activate the continuously vibrating molecules around us… and that dear reader, is a profoundly resonant life.

WE CARRY OUR HOMES WITHIN US
THE LITTLE THINGS & OUR MENTAL PHOTO ALBUM

REFLECTION & GUIDED SELF-ASSESSMENT QUESTIONS

What are the moments that playback as vibrant movies within your mind?

_____
_____
_____
_____
_____
_____
_____
_____
_____
_____
_____
_____
_____
_____
_____
_____
_____
_____
_____
_____
_____
_____
_____
_____

If you had to live minimally, what experiences or aspects of life would you find most rewarding and poignant?

When was the last time you send a letter to a loved one or physically called a friend on the phone? How can you commit to reconnecting with others on a deep level?

Think of the last time you were truly present with someone. What did you do to keep you in the moment and focused on the other person's needs?

How do you think your life has resonated with others?

How do you want your life to resonate with others in the future?

THE DESSERT OF PRACTICE
EVERY NEW BEGINNING COMES FROM AT THE END OF ANOTHER SEASON

You've finished this book but your process of revision and renewal is just beginning! This section is dedicated to checking in with yourself, the dessert of practice, the appreciation of how far you've come on your journey to the next level of you that impacts the world with purpose. Consider the following questions around the various intervals indicated below either in this book or a journal:

How have things changed since reading this book?
What have you improved upon in your life and career?
What areas could use some work?
Have your views changed over time from the initial guided-self assessment answers that you notated?
What are you most proud of at this very moment?
What is something small you have done that resonated beyond yourself?

1 MONTH AFTER

_____
_____
_____
_____
_____
_____
_____
_____
_____
_____
_____
_____
_____
_____
_____

3 MONTHS AFTER

7 MONTHS AFTER

10 MONTHS AFTER

1 YEAR AFTER

1.5 YEARS AFTER

3 YEARS AFTER

APPENDIX A

Ain't I A Woman Too
Elizabeth A. Baker
First Published by New Music Box on August 8, 2018

The classical and contemporary music worlds have recently replaced the buzzword "collaboration" with "diversity," and that push for broader inclusion has largely centered on women. The fundamental issue with the marketing and implementation of this very important matter of inclusion is that the faces and voices in the conversation are largely those of cisgender white women.

First off, I want to recognize how inspired I am by the many women who are addressing a number of problems related to inequality in our industry—from problematic power structures to sexual harassment to equal pay for equal work disparities. I do not discount any of the efforts that these strong women have made to move all of us forward.

However, the problem comes when the voices of those speaking out about diversity are largely homogenized. The problem continues when organizations promote "diversity initiatives" using only images of cisgender white women. What these actions and inactions tell women who look like me—women of color, and individuals for whom I am an ally, including non-binary and queer women—is that our voices and, more poignantly, our faces are not welcome in this conversation. Personally, it has the effect of taking my agency as a woman away from me. When people mention the breakthroughs of women composers, I do not identify with these achievements as a part of the evolution that paves my path in the music industry. The more I talk to other women of color hailing from nations across the globe, the more I understand how the subconscious presentation of diversity framed exclusively as a "middle-class white cisgender woman's problem" has the ripple effect of silencing women of varied ethnic backgrounds and gender identities.

About a year ago, a friend and colleague in the composition world spoke to me strongly about how she felt that the music industry was inherently stacked against her as a woman. In a moment which she later described to me as a "much needed check of her privilege," I explained to her that while the world might seem difficult for her as a woman, as a black woman I have almost nothing going for me... and every small task is a fight for survival in this new music world.

As the daughter of a British mum and an African-American father, my childhood was largely influenced by my mum's continental culture. I spent a great deal of my time in the family room listening to recordings of Stravinsky's Rite of Spring and wearing out countless cassette recordings of Peter and the Wolf. My father, who was determined to give me all the resources that he could, sent me to Dale Carnegie executive training courses with upwardly mobile employees of Fortune 500 companies, while other preteens whirled around in the fanciful teacups at Disney World. At the same time that I was afforded all this privilege in my youth, I was in touch with those from humbler means, as both of my parents wanted to instill within me the idea that I learn to serve others and to be grateful for whatever I was blessed to have in my life.

While my childhood was sprinkled with the privilege of the pre-recession upper middle-class, there was still a disparity. Every time I walked outside my home and had to stand on my own without the back up of my parents, I was challenged. My parents frequently had to come to school to meet with administrators and teachers who thought that I was cheating on my papers because my command of the English language was far above my grade level. If I had been a white male child, they would likely have called me a prodigy. Instead, I was tested, writing essays under time and pressure by hand on notebook paper, with the same results each time. My vernacular and writing style were not influenced by anyone but the inner voice, which sought to express my being in the most artistic and factual manner possible.

I constantly heard from my white friends, "You're black, but you aren't really black." But I was definitely black enough to be kept waiting as a child at a diner in Georgia while white patron after white patron was served before me for more than three hours. I was definitely black enough to be called a gorilla, a beast, a man, and a whole host of denigrating terms when I developed a muscular build akin to Serena Williams. I was definitely black enough to be told by multiple men throughout my life that I wasn't "classically beautiful" and that "if only you were white with blonde hair" then I would be desirable. I was definitely black enough to be told that having people steal my music wasn't a big deal because it had been happening to blacks for generations.

When I made the decision to pursue music, I understood at my core that I did not want to fall into the stereotypes of what "black music" was expected to sound like. I knew that my natural form of expression had another voice that deserved to be cultivated. I knew that focusing on a "classical" practice exploiting Negro spirituals would feel forced and disconnected from the Roman Catholic faith that was integral to my rearing. I often found myself recoiling into the works of John Cage, Morton Feldman, Arvo Pärt, and Arnold Schoenberg. I was a frequent loner in music school because my tracks were largely independently driven. These men gave me a place to start experimenting with a different voice. Then one day, I met a friend and colleague who would change my life in more ways than I could imagine—a person who challenged me to question my perceptions of how I was treated, making me realize that I deserved more basic respect than others were giving me in my personal and professional life; a person who made me realize that the only way to be the truest artist and most authentic version of myself would be to embrace all parts of myself, to put in the work to better myself, but to accept my humanity and stop beating myself up for not being the perfect little black girl everyone wanted me to be; and, most importantly, the person who introduced me to the work of Pamela Z.

When I first saw Pamela Z perform on YouTube, I cried.

I cried because her work is so beautiful, so powerful, so genuine that it touches the soul.

I cried because I saw the possibility of organic expression coming out of a setup that integrated electronics.

I cried because for the first time, I saw someone who looked like me expressing themselves freely, breaking the bonds of expectations that have been cast on our people for hundreds of years.

I often present experimental music workshops at schools throughout the U.S. I do this for a number of reasons, but the first being that when I step out onto a concert stage to play piano, the sonic expectation that my skin color and afro send the crowd is one deeply rooted in the traditions of Nina Simone and Alicia Keys. While I am grateful for the work that these women have done to pave the way for black women to be on the stage at all, I want to push the expectations of what black performers—and in particular, what black women—are expected to release into the sonic ecosystem of the concert hall.

When I inadvertently checked my colleague's privilege, I brought up the point that as a black woman in experimental music or contemporary concert music in the United States, I do not fit in anywhere.

In 21st-century America, white presenters in cosmopolitan cities have told me that they do not feel as though a black woman playing piano and electronics would fill the house enough to warrant them turning the lights on for a performance.

Meanwhile, an administrator from an African-American history museum informed me that they would be cancelling my Black History Month presentation because they did not feel as though my music was "black music" and furthermore, that it was "inaccessible for regular society."

So now as a black woman who composes and performs, I am faced with hard barriers to pursue a career in a field that I love, a field that has saved my life in difficult times, a field that has given my life meaning and purpose, space and tones that have been my blanket as I cried myself to sleep wishing that I could wake up and be a pretty white girl with all the promise and possibilities in the world in front of her.

When we leave people out of important conversations about diversity, we are creating hard barriers to inclusion. Leaving politics aside for a moment, how would it look to have the United Nations governed solely by the most Anglicized countries in the world, with absolutely no representation from Third World countries and those with more ethnically varied populations? You couldn't exactly in good conscious call it the United Nations.

We are at a cross roads in the evolution of modern music. With the advent of resources like Rob Deemer's Composer Diversity Database, we have the ability to reach out to others who are cut from a different cloth and to include their powerful voices and perspectives in the difficult conversations that we are having now about how to move forward. There should not be a conference where I am the "token black person." There should not be a festival where people of color are afraid to participate because they fear that their essence will be misappropriated by white people who fetishize the "exotic." Non-binary and queer individuals should not feel as though their very valid points about exclusionary practices centered on culture and gender identity are systematically being brushed aside or otherwise silenced by people and organizations at the top of the power structure food chain; ultimately reinforcing additional hard barriers to participation in the upper echelon of our industry. When we see a poster for a new "diversity initiative," it had better be a rainbow of skin tones and no professional model stand-ins because "you couldn't find a real composer of color." When I look up major festivals of new music, I don't want to hear that the lineup is whitewashed because "good black composers don't exist." And the most controversial of all, I don't want to hear that "black people lack a place at the table of the diversity conversation because they are just falling into line with what Western Europeans have taught them."

We can do better.

We can do better for ancestors.

We can do better for ourselves.

We can do better for future generations.

We can start today.

MANIFESTO

Elizabeth A. Baker
First Published by Aerocade Music as a part of Quadrivium in May 2018

People that promote exclusivity in the presentation and dissemination of modern concert music (art in general) are a cheque that I cannot co-sign.

Exclusivity is forged when barriers are created to art with regards to socioeconomic resources, programming that under-represents people of colour and LGBTQ+ individuals, the presence of controlled substances, the use of institutions that have historically made it difficult for any particular sect of the population to engage with art, and presentation which does not accommodate those with varying exceptionalities.

The problem is that in trying to create "trendy" or "curated" experiences to entice people to attend artistic presentations, exclusivity is often created by well meaning individuals. Art belongs to all mankind, to propagate barriers willingly or unwittingly is to hinder the progression of our species; to hinder future generations; to perpetuate the cycle of poverty... and all of these, are cheques that I cannot co-sign.

An important aside is that when programming underrepresented individuals, it is crucial to understand that artists should not be pigeonholed into only expressing the minority/LGBTQ+ narrative... while minority and sexual identities certainly inform an artistic expression, they do not define it.

The Importance of Rejection
Elizabeth A. Baker

First Published on impactreturns.org for Creative Pinellas in fulfilment of the terms of the 2017 Individual Artist Grant, on November 08, 2017

Part of being a working artist is continually submitting applications and proposals for various festivals, gigs, tours, press, residencies, commissions, and auditioning for other opportunities.

Composers submit to countless calls for scores and performers send innumerable inquires to programmers every year. The music world is incredibly small... three degrees of separation is a reality. This is where one has to form a certain resilience, because rejection is a healthy part of this life.

A few months ago, I sat in during the Creative Pinellas review panel for the Emerging Artist Grant, I saw the hurt and devastation on the faces of young artists as the panel gave them criticism; some did not take the review process well. I had a vitriol reaction and wanted desperately to scream, "You are getting reasons as to why your score is coming out a certain way, please be grateful!" In the big bad world, for those of us that make our living as freelancers, rejection often comes without reasons that we can tangibly consider. When reasons are offered it is like a ballast in rough seas, we have something to shoot towards; whether or not we decide to follow the suggestions of the reviewers, we are given an insight to how other people outside of our circle view our work.

Rejection serves another, perhaps more important purpose. It keeps our heads level. It pounds into our minds, humility. It keeps our egos in check. It makes us grateful for what we do receive, and prevents feelings of entitlement.

Often these days, little pockets form within communities... there are the favorites of local programmers and what happens is over-saturation of the marketplace. New voices feel stifled and hopeless because people don't think about calling those outside of their immediate circle.
And what happens when people forget to reach outside of their immediate circle?

In Florida there have been several complaints about experimental music events, in which female identifying and non-binary individuals are not included... events that are largely dominated by cisgender white men. While some of the organizing individuals likely do have ill-intent in their hearts, many men organizing these ensembles or performances are simply forgetting to reach outside of their circles; they don't think about the importance of inclusivity because all their "bros" look the same. It is hard to see the need for diversity, if you aren't surrounded by diversity.

The other fallout of rejection is quality. A mentor of mine recently coined the term "proficient amateurs." There are many of these in our communities and they serve an important purpose, to promote the fact that all people should have participation in the arts at some level. The problem with the boundless surfeit of proficient amateurs, particularly in less metropolitan areas, is that people are unable to discern the difference between a skilled amateur, and a professional that has truly spent time honing their craft and committing themselves to a career in the arts. Why is the bar of excellence so high in NYC, Berlin, San Francisco, Paris, and other strongholds of professional music/art? Because there is an intense level of competition, that means everyone is dealing with rejection and everyone is aware that they are on some level replaceable. This culture, while intensely stressful, causes one to either push themselves to reach and exceed the bar set locally, or to form their own artistic identity separate and perhaps in response to the stressors around them.

The general point is that rejection, when viewed through positive eyes, pushes us to be better artists and better people. Rejection is not a complete shutdown of our dreams, but rather inspiration to conquer barriers, including the ones within ourselves.

PLEASE DON'T CALL ME A COMPOSER, CLASSICAL MUSICIAN, TOY PIANIST...

Elizabeth A. Baker

First Published on Elizabeth A. Baker's Official Website on July 26, 2016

A strange thing happened to me recently, I was introduced to someone in conversation as a "composer" and immediately, I felt an oppressive set of walls rapidly closing in on my soul. I felt artistically constrained by the meaning of the word "composer" but moreover I felt that in assigning this label to my person, that I was betraying the other parts of my creative self. I've always had my hand in a lot of different media and each one has brought me a sense of centeredness.

Pianist. Toy Pianist. Author. Composer. Engineer. Lecturer. Non-Profit Administrator. Arts Entrepreneur. The list has been growing rapidly and it still doesn't feel like an accurate representation of who I am as a woman, let alone as an artist. We live in a world where "branding" is a reality due to an increasingly commercialized society, which creates a problematic situation whereby I have to create a definition for my body of work. For the past several months, I have been turning over ideas of a group of words that would succinctly describe my current place artistically, but would afford enough flexibility in meaning that I would not feel the dark foreboding walls surrounding me for quite some time, if ever again.

I thought about calling myself a "multimedia artist" but that rings with so many connotations of a visual body of work, particularly a digital media portfolio, that I wrestled for weeks with trying to accept the term. Eventually, an epiphany... New Renaissance Artist!

The word renaissance as most adults may recall from grade school history class, signals rebirth and revival. Historically, the term Renaissance has referred to people who were well versed in a vast array of subjects including art, philosophy, science, and literature. As an artist and personally, I feel as though I am constantly going through a revival, a transformation, and a rebirth. I'm always looking to push myself further in my sonic practice but along the way I become fascinated with other subjects that I may or may not have studied previously. I return to old subjects with a new outlook. Infamously, one of my mentors declared "...most people change their molecules every seven years. Elizabeth changes her molecules every seven months." While

Renaissance may conjure images of dusty Renaissance fairs, with people in ornate costumes and giant turkey legs, my purpose in prefacing Renaissance with New, is to signal that we are and I am in a place for a fresh look at revival. There have been many other Renaissance periods, including the Harlem Renaissance (which as an African-American woman, I can identify deeply with from an artistic standpoint.), but my purpose is to embrace the term away from geographical or chronological prejudice. I am a New Renaissance Artist. I embrace a constant stream of change and rebirth in my practice, which expands into a variety of media, chiefly an exploration of how the sonic world can be manipulated to personify a variety of philosophies and principles both tangible as well as intangible.

A change is coming and by the end of the 2016, I hope to have fully integrated this new description of myself. I am now asking anyone seeking to speak or write, about me with the new identification of New Renaissance Artist. I've kept this secret for several weeks, as I wanted to be sure that this was the right course of action. I can safely say that the change has been immediate. I feel open to new possibilities. The walls have come crashing down, and a forest of vibrant colors surrounds me with new places waiting to be explored. A fresh spring breeze encircles me, and I feel as though I can finally breathe artistically.

Elizabeth A. Baker – New Renaissance Artist

APPENDIX B
SELECTED RESOURCES & FURTHER READING

Ochs, Larry. "RADAR and Rova's Development of Language for Structured Improvisation ." Rova:Arts, Rova Saxophone Quartet, 1999, www.rova.org/foodforthought/radar.html?fbclid=IwAR0EYgio1pZVFTPk3-2sV37z0qy82YjC9PIAwLXNV3aBLOP0z5oclFoK4tU.

Pavitra, K. S., C. R. Chandrashekar, and Partha Choudhury. "Creativity and Mental Health: A Profile of Writers and Musicians." Indian Journal of Psychiatry 49.1 (2007): 34-43. PMC. Web. 11 Oct. 2018.

Matei, Raluca, and Jane Ginsborg. "Music Performance Anxiety in Classical Musicians - What We Know about What Works." BJPsych International 14.2 (2017): 33-35. Print.

Dredge, Stuart. "Wellbeing in the Music Industry: 'It's a Global Myth That Mental Illness Is a Weakness.'" Music:)Ally, Music Ally Ltd., 8 Feb. 2018, musically.com/2018/02/08/wellbeing-music-industry-mental-illness/.

Valentish, Jenny. " Perfectionism and Poverty: Why Musicians Struggle with Mental Health." The Guardian, Guardian News and Media Limited, 19 July 2018, 2221, www.theguardian.com/music/2018/jun/20/perfectionism-and-poverty-why-musicians-struggle-with-mental-health.

"Hirsutism: evaluation and treatment" Indian journal of dermatology vol. 55,1 (2010): 3-7. https://www.ncbi.nlm.nih.gov/pmc/articles/PMC2856356/

Lipton MG, Sherr L, Elford J, Rustin MH, Clayton WJ. Women living with facial hair: the psychological and behavioral burden. J Psychosom Res. 2006 Aug;61(2):161-8. PubMed PMID: 16880018. https://www.ncbi.nlm.nih.gov/pubmed/16880018

Wing Sue, Derald. "Microaggressions: More than Just Race." Psychology Today, Sussex Publishers, Nov. 2010, www.psychologytoday.com/us/blog/microaggressions-in-everyday-life/201011/microaggressions-more-just-race.

Rosenberg, Steven A, et al. "Cancer Immunotherapy: Moving beyond Current Vaccines." Nature News, Nature Publishing Group, 1 Sept. 2004, www.nature.com/articles/nm1100.

Williams Crenshaw, Kimberlé, et al. BLACK GIRLS MATTER: PUSHED OUT, OVERPOLICED AND UNDERPROTECTED. African American Policy Forum, 2015, pp. 1-53, BLACK GIRLS MATTER: PUSHED OUT, OVERPOLICED AND UNDERPROTECTED.

Epstein, Rebecca, et al. Girlhood Interrupted: The Erasure of Black Girls' Childhood. Georgetown Law Center on Poverty and Inequality, 2017, pp. 1-23, Girlhood Interrupted: The Erasure of Black Girls' Childhood.

Frank, Dana L et al. "Biofeedback in medicine: who, when, why and how?" Mental health in family medicine vol. 7,2 (2010): 85-91.

APPENDIX C
FURTHER LISTENING

The following are a collection of recordings that have meant a lot to me over the years, and I present them here for the reader to become a listener inside my mind.

Mellow Waves by Cornelius
cornelius.storenvy.com/collections/1518050-mellow-waves

Untitled by Jitters
jittersmusic.bandcamp.com/album/untitled

Nude Beach by Nude Tayne
nudetayne.bandcamp.com/album/nude-beach

LOCI by Sean Hamilton
sean-hamilton.bandcamp.com/album/loci

Pamela Z: A Delay Is Better by Pamela Z
www.pamelaz.com/recordings.html

Quadrivium by Elizabeth A. Baker
elizabethabaker.bandcamp.com/album/quadrivium

{a series of strange narratives} by Elizabeth A. Baker
elizabethabaker.bandcamp.com/album/a-series-of-strange-narratives

{this is not a piano album} by Elizabeth A. Baker
elizabethabaker.bandcamp.com/album/this-is-not-a-piano-album

Hamilton/Suarez Duo by Sean Hamilton & Leo Suarez
leosuarez.bandcamp.com/album/hamilton-suarez-duo

Hardcore Boring Electronic Music Vol 1 by Nathan Corder
nathancorder.bandcamp.com/album/hardcore-boring-electronic-music-vol-1

Leo's Song by Suitcases of Sound
suitcasesofsound.bandcamp.com/track/leos-song-3

Vesper by I And I
iandi.bandcamp.com/album/vesper

The Self Titled Album Shansa Barsnaan by Shatner's Bassoon
shatnersbassoonband.bandcamp.com/album/the-self-titled-album-shansa-barsnaan

Helmut Lachenmann: Chamber Music
Michael Bach (cello), David Smeyers (clarinet),
Bernhard Wambach (piano)
www.prestomusic.com/classical/products/8033196--lachenmann-chamber-music

COWELL: Homage to Iran / Piano Pieces / Set of Five / Six Casual Developments / Two Songs by Continuum Ensemble
www.naxos.com/catalogue/item.asp?item_code=8.559193

Gesualdo: Madrigals, Books 5 & 6 by Delitiae Musicae
www.arkivmusic.com/classical/album.jsp?album_id=937704

I Saw The Devil Last Night And Now The Sun Shines Bright by Moros Eros
www.victorymerch.com/merch/cds/9320/moros-eros-i-saw-the-devil-last-night-and-now-the-sun-shines-bright-cd

Jealous Me Was Killed By Curiosity by Moros Eros
www.victorymerch.com/merch/cds/11479/moros-eros-jealous-me-was-killed-by-curiosity-cd

Thom Yorke / Atoms for Peace
store-us.wasteheadquarters.com/collections/thom-yorke-atoms-for-peace

mouse on the keys
mouseonthekeys.net

SPECIAL THANKS

To all who have contributed to my journey -

To all who have doubted my abilities -

To all who have supported me unwaveringly -

To all who have attempted to sabotage my purpose -

To all who have shown me great loyalty -

To all who have shared unconditional love -

To all who have entered my life in both positive and negative ways -

I am grateful for every breath and all the energy that has made me into the strong centred woman that I am today. I look forward to a future full of more lessons, laughter, love, heartache, and well... life.

CPSIA information can be obtained
at www.ICGtesting.com
Printed in the USA
LVHW091433310319
612448LV00001B/89/P